POOR JEWS

POOR JEWS:

An American Awakening

edited by Naomi Levine
and Martin Hochbaum

Transaction Books
New Brunswick, New Jersey

Library of Congress Catalogue Number:
ISBN: 0–87855–073–9 (cloth); 0–87855–570–6 (paper)

ACKNOWLEDGMENTS

Grateful acknowledgment is made to the following authors and publishers for permission to reprint selections:

Oscar Lewis, "The Culture of Poverty," from *La Vida*, by Oscar Lewis. Copyright © 1965, 1966 by Oscar Lewis. Reprinted by permission of Random House, Inc.

Ann G. Wolfe, "The Invisible Jewish Poor," from "The Invisible Jewish Poor," in *Journal of Jewish Communal Services,* 48 (1972) 3:259–65.

Paul Cowan, "Jews Without Money, Revisited," from *The Village Voice.* Copyrighted © 1972 by The Village Voice, Inc.,
Phyllis Franck, "The Hasidic Poor in New York City," is reprinted by permission of the Office of Economic Opportunity from Phyllis Franck, "On Being Hasidic in New York City," in *Vista,* Vol. 5, No. 2 (February 1969): 24–30.

Isadore Twersky, "Some Aspects of the Jewish Attitude Toward the Welfare State," from "Some Aspects of the Jewish Attitude Toward the Welfare State," pp. 221–42, in *A Treasury of Tradition*, edited by Norman Lamm and Walter J. Wurzburger (New York: Hebrew Publishing Company, 1967).

Leo Jung, "Concept of Tzedakah in Contemporary Jewish Life," from "Concept of Tzedakah in Contemporary Jewish Life," in *The Rabbi and the Jewish Social Worker,* edited by Rabbi Morris N. Kertzer (New York: Commission on Synagogue Relations, Federation of Jewish Philanthropies, 1972).

Aviva Silberman, "Problems in Serving Chicago's Jewish Poor," from *Who Are the Jewish Poor?* (Chicago: The Ark, 1971).

William Kavesh, "The Jewish Hospital and the Jewish Community," from "The Jewish Hospital and the Jewish Community," vol. 5, no. 37, (1972) of *Response: A Contemporary Jewish Review.*

Bruno Stein, "A Systematic Approach to Poverty Policy," from Chapter 5 of *On Relief: The Economics of Poverty and Public Welfare* by Bruno Stein, copyright 1971 by Basic Books, Inc.

"Elder's Lib", Editorial of December 1, 1971, © 1971 by the New York Times Company. Reprinted by Permission.

Contents

Preface   ix

Introduction   Naomi Levine and Martin Hochbaum   1

1. POVERTY AMONG JEWS

The Culture of Poverty   Oscar Lewis   9

The Invisible Jewish Poor   Ann G. Wolfe   26

Jews Without Money, Revisited   Paul Cowan   39

The Hasidic Poor in New York City   Phyllis Franck   59

2. THE JEWISH RESPONSE TO THE JEWISH POOR

Some Aspects of the Jewish Attitude
Toward the Welfare State   Isadore Twersky   73

Concept of Tzedakah in Contemporary Jewish Life
Leo Jung   96

Our Jewish Poor:
How Can They Be Served?   Jerome M. Comar   105

Problems in Serving Chicago's Jewish Poor
Aviva Silberman   118

3. THE JEWISH POOR AND THE WAR AGAINST POVERTY

Why Jews Get Less: A Study of Jewish Participation in the
Poverty Program
Naomi Levine and Martin Hochbaum   135

Memorandum of Inspection Division   Office of Economic
Opportunity   148

Re: Jewish Poverty
Sol Levy and Bernard Weinberger   154

4. ON ENDING JEWISH POVERTY

The Jewish Hospital and the Jewish Community
Wiliam Kavesh   167

A Systematic Approach to Poverty Policy
Bruno Stein   185

Postscript: Elder's Lib   *New York Times*   200

Contributors   204

Index   205

Preface

The efforts of a number of people made possible the publication of this book. We are grateful to the authors and publishers who consented to the republication of their work. Additionally, the membership and staff of the American Jewish Congress provided us with constant encouragement. We are also appreciative of the efforts of Jack D. Weiler, a true friend of the Jewish poor.

Naturally, any errors or shortcomings in this volume are exclusively our own.

Introduction

Most people think that America's Jewish population consists entirely of middle and upper-middle income people. It has recently become clear, however, that this image of Jewish "affluence" is a distortion of the facts. The truth is that, as is the case with every other ethnic group in America, there are large numbers of impoverished Jews with incomes below the established poverty level, and large numbers of working-class Jews are employed in relatively low paying manual and white-collar jobs.

There are several reasons why the existence of the Jewish poor has been virtually unknown until recently. The basic reason is that no comprehensive private or public study of the income of the American Jewish population has yet been made. Indeed, even the United States Census Bureau has not gathered this information. In addition, the limited available data on this subject is frequently misinterpreted. For example, a 1970 survey of Jewish college freshmen in America demonstrates that the parents of Jewish college freshmen are more than twice as likely to earn more than $15,000 per year as are the parents of non-Jewish college freshmen. The readers of these aggregate figures, impressed with the large percentage of Jews earning moderately good salaries, often forget that they hide the existence of a significant number of impoverished Jews at the lower end of the economic scale.

As an important step toward overcoming this lack of data, we welcome the recent statistical analysis released in January, 1973, by the Federation of Jewish Philanthropies of New York, entitled "New York's Jewish Poor and Jewish Working Class: Economic Status and Social Needs." The research for this study was undertaken by the Center for New York City Affairs of the New School for Social Research. It is an important and long overdue addition to the current efforts at understanding the scope and demography of the Jewish poor.

The major findings of this report are:

1. 272,000 individuals, or 15.1 percent of the Jewish population of 1.8 million in New York, are poor or near poor. This figure includes 191,000 poor Jews and 81,000 who are near poor; 2. 190,300 families totaling 432,000 individuals are between the near poverty level and what the Bureau of Labor Statistics calls a moderate level of living. This is almost one quarter of New York City's Jewish population, and constitutes the Jewish working class.

Since almost one third of the Jews in the United States live in the New York area, and since the problems of Jews in New York City are not significantly different from the problems of inner city Jews in other large metropolitan areas, these statistics have national implications.

The traditional Jewish pride, which prevents many poor Jews from seeking out the public and private services to which they are entitled, is another reason why it has been difficult to identify poor Jews. A typical incident relating to this problem occurred recently in a poverty neighborhood in New York City. In answer to a question by the editors regarding the extent of Jewish participation in various poverty programs, an Orthodox rabbi stated that he was unaware of any Jewish participation. When he was asked why this was the case, since he had just observed that there were large numbers of improverished Jews in his area, he replied, "Thank heavens, our people have pride."

And those Jews that do seek assistance generally prefer to use Jewish charities (although such charities as the Federation of Jewish Philanthropies depend on public financing for well over 90 percent of their operating expenses). Their absence from the roles of the public charities, and the mistaken notion that the Jews "are taking care of their own," add to the general impression that there are few poor Jews, and that those who exist are being adequately cared for by the Jewish community. Nothing could be further from the truth.

The fact that perhaps two thirds of poor Jews are over age 60 is another distinguishing demographic statistic about Jewish poverty in America. This figure contrasts with the general population, where approximately 75 percent of the poor people are under 60 years of age. For example, in the South Beach area of Miami Beach, there are 40,000 poor residents. Four fifths of them are over 65, and 85 percent of them are Jewish, with an average annual income of under $2,500. According to one of the articles in this compilation, "The Invisible Jewish Poor," thousands of these people live on less than $28 per week for food and rent. Similarly, in New York City, there are approximately 86,000 elderly poor Jews living in 15 of the city's 26 designated poverty areas, and at least another 25,000 elderly poor live outside these poverty areas. Thus out of a total of 191,000 poor Jews in New York City, 111,000—or almost 60 percent—are aged.

The problems of the poor elderly Jews who reside in the inner city go beyond what are traditionally perceived as the problems of the aged poor—low income, poor health, abominable housing accommodations and loneliness. In addition, these people frequently find themselves living in a religiously hostile environment. The institutions that they have always known—synagogues, kosher butcher stores, etc.—have long since disappeared. The knock on the door is viewed, not as the beginning of a visit by a friend or neighbor, but as the attempt of a dope addict planning to burglarize their apartment to determine whether anyone is home. Feelings of abandonment and fear are widespread among these aged Jews, and many of them are little more than prisoners within their own homes.

The remaining one third of the Jewish poor are single individuals, families with children and families with only one parent. As with the aged, this group often finds that it is living within a hostile environment. The major differences between these two groups of poor Jews is in the area of needs. While both groups need better housing, medical attention and a plethora of other service, the younger impoverished Jews need more education, manpower training programs and job referrals.

Intermingled with both the young and the aged poor are the Hasidic Jews. They are a community with large numbers of poor people and with other, special problems. The difficulty they face in finding employment that permits them strictly to observe their religious beliefs has seriously impaired their ability to support themselves above the poverty level. They are generally found in neighborhoods that were once Jewish, but that today are undergoing rapid change. Most of them are concentrated in two sections in the Borough of Brooklyn in New York City.

The problems of impoverished Jews are both similar to and different from the problems of the non-Jewish poor. Together with the other poor, they share such problems as inadequate diet, poor health, dilapidated apartments and fear brought on by their frequent location in neighborhoods that have an unusually high crime rate.

There are, however, certain problems of the Jewish poor that result from their religious beliefs. The need to keep a kosher home and purchase special foods for holidays obviously increases the cost of the family's food bill.

Furthermore, many of the poor Jews, for religious reasons, send their children to private religious schools, which means a monthly payment for their education. Among Orthodox and Hasidic Jews, their religious beliefs prohibit the use of birth control to limit the size of the family.

The authors recognized at the outset that the problem of poor Jews and non-Jews cannot be solved by private philanthropy alone. For the most part, help must come from more extensive government aid—through increased social security benefits, more adequate health and hospital benefits, increased minimum wages, better living accommodations and other social and economic measures that will serve, both to aid the poor in their ability to climb out of poverty, and to aid those who are unable to work to live more fulfilling lives.

The pursuit of these goals for all persons, Jewish and non-Jewish, must become a major concern of the total community. At the same time, it is hoped that the entire Jewish community and its agencies will focus on the special problems of the Jewish poor—a problem that until recently has been lamentably neglected.

1. POVERTY AMONG JEWS

The Culture of Poverty
Oscar Lewis

. . . Although a great deal has been written about poverty and the poor, the concept of a culture of poverty is relatively new. I first suggested it in 1959 in my book *Five Families: Mexican Case Studies in the Culture of Poverty.* The phrase is a catchy one and has become widely used and misused. [1] Michael Harrington used it extensively in his book *The Other America* (1961), which played an important role in sparking the national anti-poverty program in the United States. However, he used it in a somewhat broader and less technical sense than I had intended. I shall try to define it more precisely as a conceptual model, with special emphasis upon the distinction between poverty and the culture of poverty. The absence of intensive anthropological studies of poor families from a wide variety of national and cultural contexts and especially from the socialist countries, is a serious handicap in formulating valid crosscultural regularities. The model presented here is therefore provisional and subject to modification as new studies become available.

Throughout recorded history, in literature, in proverbs and in popular sayings, we find two opposite evaluations of the nature of the poor. Some characterize the poor as blessed, virtuous, upright, serene, independent, honest, kind and happy. Others characterize them as evil, mean, violent, sordid and criminal. These contradictory and confusing evaluations are also reflected in the in-fighting that is going on in the current war against poverty. Some stress the great potential of the poor for self-help, leadership and community organization, while others point to the sometimes irreversible, destructive effect of poverty upon individual character, and therefore emphasize the need for guidance and control to remain in the hands of the middle class, which presumably has better mental health.

These opposing views reflect a political power struggle between competing groups. However, some of the confusion results from the failure to distinguish between poverty per se and the culture of poverty, and the tendency to focus upon the individual personality rather than upon the group—that is, the family and the slum community.

As an anthropologist I have tried to understand poverty and its associated traits as a culture or, more accurately, as a subculture[2] with its own structure and rationale, as a way of life which is passed down from generation to generation along family lines. This view directs attention to the fact that the culture of poverty in modern nations is not only a matter of economic deprivation, of disorganization or of the absence of something. It is also something positive, and provides some rewards without which the poor could hardly carry on.

Elsewhere I have suggested that the culture of poverty transcends regional, rural-urban and national differences and shows remarkable similarities in family structure, interpersonal relations, time orientation, value systems and spending patterns. These cross-national similarities are examples of independent invention and convergence. They are common adaptations to common problems.

The culture of poverty can come into being in a variety of historical contexts. However, it tends to grow and flourish in societies with the following set of conditions: a cash economy, wage labor and production for profit; a persistently high rate of unemployment and underemployment for unskilled labor; low wages; the failure to provide social, political and economic organization, either on a voluntary basis or by government imposition, for the low-income population; the existence of a bilateral kinship system rather than a unilateral one[3]; and finally, the existence of a set of values in the dominant class which stresses the accumulation of wealth and property, the possibility of upward mobility and thrift, and explains low economic status as the result of personal inadequacy or inferiority.

The way of life which develops among some of the poor under these conditions is the culture of poverty. It can best be studied in urban or rural slums and can be described in terms of some interrelated social, economic and psychological traits.[4] However, the number of traits and the relationships between them may vary from society to society and from family to family. For example, in a highly literate society, illiteracy may be more diagnostic of the culture of poverty than in a society where illiteracy is widespread and where even the well-to-do may be illiterate, as in some Mexican peasant villages before the revolution.

The culture of poverty is both an adaptation and a reaction of the poor to their marginal position in a class-stratified, highly individuated, capitalistic society. It represents an effort to cope with feelings of hopelessness and despair which develop from the realization of the improbability of achieving success in terms of the values and goals of the larger society. Indeed, many of the traits of the culture of poverty can be viewed as attempts at local solutions for problems not met by existing institutions and agencies because the people are not eligible for them, cannot afford them, or are ignorant or suspicious of them. For example, unable to obtain credit from banks, they are thrown upon their own resources and organize informal credit devices without interest.

The culture of poverty, however, is not only an adaptation to a set of objective conditions of the larger society. Once it comes into existence it tends to perpetuate itself from generation to generation, because of its effect on the children. By the time slum children are age six or seven, they have usually absorbed the basic values and attitudes of their subculture and are not psychologically geared to take full advantage of changing conditions or increased opportunities which may occur in their lifetime.

Most frequently the culture of poverty develops when a stratified social and economic system is breaking down or is being replaced by another, as in the case of the transition from feudalism to capitalism or during periods of rapid technological change. Often it results from imperial conquest in which the native social and economic structure is smashed and the natives are maintained in a servile colonial status, sometimes for many generations. It can also occur in the process of detribalization, such as that going on in Africa.

The most likely candidates for the culture of poverty are the people who come from the lower strata of a rapidly changing society and are already partially alienated from it. Thus landless rural workers who migrate to the cities can be expected to develop a culture of poverty much more readily than migrants from stable peasant villages with a well-organized traditional culture. In this connection there is a striking contrast between Latin America, where the rural population long ago made the transition from a tribal to a peasant society, and Africa, which is still close to its tribal heritage. The more corporate nature of many of the African tribal societies, in contrast to Latin American rural communities, and the persistence of village ties tend to inhibit or delay the formation of a full-blown culture of poverty in many of the African towns and cities. The special conditions of apartheid in South Africa, where the migrants are segregated into separate "locations" and do not enjoy freedom of movement, create special problems. Here the institutionalization of repression and discrimination tend to develop a greater sense of identity and group consciousness.

The culture of poverty can be studied from various points of view: the relationship between the subculture and the larger society; the nature of the slum community; the nature of the family; and the attitudes, values and character structure of the individual.

The lack of effective participation and integration of the poor in the major institutions of the larger society is one of the crucial characteristics of the culture of poverty. This is a complex matter and results from a variety of factors which may include lack of economic resources, segregation and discrimination, fear, suspicion or apathy, and the development of local solutions for problems. However, "participation" in some of the institutions of the larger society—for example, in the jails, the army and the public relief system —does not per se eliminate the traits of the culture of poverty. In the case of a relief system which barely keeps people alive, both the basic poverty and the sense of hopelessness are perpetuated rather than eliminated.

Low wages, chronic unemployment and underemployment lead to low income, lack of property ownership, absence of savings, absence of food reserves in the home, and a chronic shortage of cash. These conditions reduce the possibility of effective participation in the larger economic system. And as a response to these conditions we find in the culture of poverty a high incidence of pawning of personal goods, borrowing from local moneylenders at usurious rates of interest, spontaneous informal credit devices organized by neighbors, the use of secondhand clothing and furniture, and the pattern of frequent buying of small quantities of food many times a day as the need arises.

People with a culture of poverty produce very little

wealth and receive very little in return. They have a low level of literacy and education, usually do not belong to labor unions, are not members of political parties, generally do not participate in the national welfare agencies, and make very little use of banks, hospitals, department stores, museums or art galleries. They have a critical attitude toward some of the basic institutions of the dominant classes, hatred of the police, mistrust of government and those in high position, and a cynicism which extends even to the church. This gives the culture of poverty a high potential for protest and for being used in political movements aimed against the existing social order.

People with a culture of poverty are aware of middle-class values, talk about them and even claim some of them as their own, but on the whole they do not live by them. Thus it is important to distinguish between what they say and what they do. For example, many will tell you that marriage by law, by the church, or by both, is the ideal form of marriage, but few will marry. To men who have no steady jobs or other sources of income, who do not own property and have no wealth to pass on to their children, who are present-time oriented and who want to avoid the expense and legal difficulties involved in formal marriage and divorce, free unions or consensual marriage makes a lot of sense. Women will often turn down offers of marriage because they feel it ties them down to men who are immature, punishing and generally unreliable. Women feel that consensual union gives them a better break; it gives them some of the freedom and flexibility that men have. By not giving the fathers of their children legal status as husbands, the women have a stronger claim on their children if they decide to leave their men. It also gives women exclusive rights to a house or any other property they may own.

When we look at the culture of poverty on the local community level, we find poor housing conditions, crowding, gregariousness, but above all a minimum of organization beyond the level of the nuclear and extended family. Occasionally there are informal, temporary group-ings or voluntary associations within slums. The existence of neighborhood gangs which cut across slum settle-ments represents a considerable advance beyond the zero point of the continuum that I have in mind. Indeed, it is the low level of organization which gives the culture of poverty its marginal and anachronistic quality in our highly complex, specialized, organized society. Most primitive peoples have achieved a higher level of socio-cultural organization than our modern urban slum dwellers.

In spite of the generally low level of organization, there may be a sense of community and esprit de corps in urban slums and in slum neighborhoods. This can vary within a single city, or from region to region or country to country. The major factors influencing this variation are the size of the slum, its location and physical characteristics, length of residence, incidence of home and landownership (versus squatter rights), rentals, ethnicity, kinship ties, and freedom or lack of freedom of movement. When slums are separated from the surrounding area by enclosing walls or other physical barriers, when rents are low and fixed and stability of residence is great (twenty or thirty years), when the population constitutes a distinct ethnic, racial or language group, is bound by ties of kinship or *compadrazgo*, and when there are some internal voluntary associations, then the sense of local community approaches that of a village community. In many cases this combination of favorable conditions does not exist. However, even where internal organization and esprit de corps is at a bare minimum and people move around a great deal, a sense of territoriality develops which sets off the slum neighborhoods from the rest of the city. In Mexico City and San Juan this sense of territoriality results from the unavailability of low-income housing outside the slum areas. In South Africa the sense of territoriality grows out of the segregation enforced by the the government, which confines the rural migrants to specific locations.

On the family level, the major traits of the culture of poverty are the absence of childhood as a specially prolonged and protected stage in the life cycle, early initiation into sex, free unions or consensual marriages, a relatively high incidence of the abandonment of wives and children, a trend toward female or mother-centered families and consequently a much greater knowledge of maternal relatives, a strong predisposition to authoritarianism, lack of privacy, verbal emphasis upon family solidarity which is only rarely achieved because of sibling rivalry, and competition for limited goods and maternal affection.

On the level of the individual the major characteristics are a strong feeling of marginality, of helplessness, of dependence and of inferiority. I found this to be true of slum dwellers in Mexico City and San Juan among families who do not constitute a distinct ethnic or racial group and who do not suffer from racial discrimination. In the United States, of course, the culture of poverty of the Negroes has the additional disadvantage of racial discrimination, but as I have already suggested, this additional disadvantage contains a great potential for revolutionary protest and organization which seems to be absent in the slums of Mexico City or among the poor whites in the South.

Other traits include a high incidence of maternal deprivation, of orality, of weak ego structure, confusion of sexual identification, a lack of impulse control, a strong present-time orientation with relatively little ability to defer gratification and to plan for the future, a sense of resignation and fatalism, a widespread belief in male superiority, and a high tolerance for psychological pathology of all sorts.

People with a culture of poverty are provincial and locally oriented and have little sense of history. They know only their own troubles, their own local conditions, their own neighborhood, their own way of life. Usually they do not have the knowledge, the vision or the ideology to see the similarities between their problems and those of their counterparts elsewhere in the world. They are not class-conscious, although they are very sensitive indeed to status distinctions.

When the poor become class-conscious or active members of trade union organizations, or when they adopt an internationalist outlook on the world, they are no longer part of the culture of poverty, although they may still be desperately poor. Any movement, be it religious, pacifist or revolutionary, which organizes and gives hope to the poor and effectively promotes solidarity and a sense of identification with larger groups, destroys the psychological and social core of the culture of poverty. In this connection, I suspect that the civil rights movement among the Negroes in the United States has done more to improve their self-image and self-respect than have their economic advances, although, without doubt, the two are mutually reinforcing.

The distinction between poverty and the culture of poverty is basic to the model described here. There are degrees of poverty and many kinds of poor people. The culture of poverty refers to one way of life shared by poor people in given historical and social contexts. The economic traits which I have listed for the culture of poverty are necessary but not sufficient to define the phenomena I have in mind. There are a number of historical examples of very poor segments of the population which do not have a way of life that I would describe as a subculture of poverty. Here I should like to give four examples:

1. Many of the primitive or preliterate peoples studied by anthropologists suffer from dire poverty which is the result of poor technology and/or poor natural resources, or of both, but they do not have the traits of the subculture of poverty. Indeed, they do not

constitute a subculture because their societies are highly stratified. In spite of their poverty they have a relatively integrated, satisfying and self-sufficient culture. Even the simplest food-gathering and hunting tribes have a considerable amount of organization, bands and band chiefs, tribal councils and local self-government—traits which are not found in the culture of poverty.

2. In India the lower castes (the Chamars, the leather workers, and the Bhangis, the sweepers) may be desperately poor, both in the villages and in the cities, but most of them are integrated into the larger society and have their own *panchayat*[5] organizations which cut across village lines and give them a considerable amount of power.[6] In addition to the caste system, which gives individuals a sense of identity and belonging, there is still another factor, the clan system. Wherever there are unilateral kinship systems or clans one would not expect to find the culture of poverty, because a clan system gives people a sense of belonging to a corporate body with a history and a life of its own, thereby providing a sense of continuity, a sense of a past and of a future.

3. The Jews of eastern Europe were very poor, but they did not have many of the traits of the culture of poverty because of their tradition of literacy, the great value placed upon learning, the organization of the community around the rabbi, the proliferation of local voluntary associations, and their religion which taught that they were the chosen people.

4. My fourth example is speculative and relates to socialism. On the basis of my limited experience in one socialist country—Cuba—and on the basis of my reading, I am inclined to believe that the culture of poverty does not exist in the socialist countries. I first went to Cuba in 1947 as a visiting professor for the

State Department. At that time I began a study of a sugar plantation in Melena del Sur and of a slum in Havana. After the Castro Revolution I made my second trip to Cuba as a correspondent for a major magazine, and I revisited the same slum and some of the same families. The physical aspect of the slum had changed very little, except for a beautiful new nursery school. It was clear that the people were still desperately poor, but I found much less of the despair, apathy and hopelessness which are so diagnostic of urban slums in the culture of poverty. They expressed great confidence in their leaders and hope for a better life in the future. The slum itself was now highly organized, with block committees, educational committees, party committees. The people had a new sense of power and importance. They were armed and were given a doctrine which glorified the lower class as the hope of humanity. (I was told by one Cuban official that they had practically eliminated delinquency by giving arms to the delinquents!)

It is my impression that the Castro regime—unlike Marx and Engels—did not write off the so-called lumpen proletariat as an inherently reactionary and anti-revolutionary force, but rather saw its revolutionary potential and tried to utilize it. In this connection, Frantz Fanon makes a similar evaluation of the role of the lumpen proletariat based upon his experience in the Algerian struggle for independence. In his recently published book[7] he wrote:

It is within this mass of humanity, this people of the shanty towns, at the core of the lumpen proletariat, that the rebellion will find its urban spearhead. For the lumpen proletariat, that horde of starving men, uprooted from their tribe and from their clan, constitutes one of the most spontaneous and most radically revolutionary forces of a colonized people.

My own studies of the urban poor in the slums of San Juan do not support the generalizations of Fanon. I have found very little revolutionary spirit or radical ideology among low-income Puerto Ricans. On the contrary, most of the families I studied were quite conservative politically and about half of them were in favor of the Republican Statehood Party. It seems to me that the revolutionary potential of people with a culture of poverty will vary considerably according to the national context and the particular historical circumstances. In a country like Algeria which was fighting for its independence, the lumpen proletariat was drawn into the struggle and became a vital force. However, in countries like Puerto Rico, in which the movement for independence has very little mass support, and in countries like Mexico which achieved their independence a long time ago and are now in their postrevolutionary period, the lumpen proletariat is not a leading source of rebellion or of revolutionary spirit.

In effect, we find that in primitive societies and in caste societies, the culture of poverty does not develop. In socialist, fascist and in highly developed capitalist societies with a welfare state, the culture of poverty tends to decline. I suspect that the culture of poverty flourishes in, and is generic to, the early free-enterprise stage of capitalism and that it is also endemic in colonialism.

It is important to distinguish between different profiles in the subculture of poverty, depending upon the national context in which these subcultures are found. If we think of the culture of poverty primarily in terms of the factor of integration in the larger society and a sense of identification with the great tradition of that society, or with a new emerging revolutionary tradition, then we will not be surprised that some slum dwellers with a lower per capita income may have moved farther away from the core characteristics of the culture of poverty than others with a higher per capita income. For example, Puerto Rico has a much higher per capita income than Mexico, yet Mexicans have a deeper sense of identity.

I have listed fatalism and a low level of aspiration as one of the key traits for the subculture of poverty. Here too, however, the national context makes a big difference. Certainly the level of aspiration of even the poorest sector of the population in a country like the United States, with its traditional ideology of upward mobility and democracy, is much higher than in more backward countries like Ecuador and Peru, where both the ideology and the actual possibilities of upward mobility are extremely limited and where authoritarian values still persist in both the urban and rural milieus.

Because of the advanced technology, high level of literacy, the development of mass media and the relatively high aspiration level of all sectors of the population, especially when compared with underdeveloped nations, I believe that although there is still a great deal of poverty in the United States (estimates range from thirty to fifty million people), there is relatively little of what I would call the culture of poverty. My rough guess would be that only about 20 percent of the population below the poverty line (between six and ten million people) in the United States have characteristics which would justify classifying their way of life as that of a culture of poverty. Probably the largest sector within this group would consist of very low-income Negroes, Mexicans, Puerto Ricans, American Indians and Southern poor whites. The relatively small number of people in the United States with a culture of poverty is a positive factor, because it is much more difficult to eliminate the culture of poverty than to eliminate poverty per se.

Middle-class people, and this would certainly include most social scientists, tend to concentrate on the negative aspects of the culture of poverty. They tend to associate negative valences to such traits as present-time orientation and concrete versus abstract orientation. I do not intend to idealize or romanticize the culture of poverty. As someone has said, "It is easier to praise poverty than to live in it"; yet some of the positive aspects which may flow from these traits must not be overlooked. Living in the present may develop a capacity for spontaneity and adventure, for the enjoyment of the sensual, the indulgence of impulse, which is often blunted in the middle-class, future-oriented man. Perhaps it is this reality of the moment which the existentialist writers are so desperately trying to recapture but which the culture of poverty experiences as natural, everyday phenomena. The frequent use of violence certainly provides a ready outlet for hostility, so that people in the culture of poverty suffer less from repression than does the middle class.

In the traditional view, anthropologists have said that culture provides human beings with a design for living, with ready-made set of solutions for human problems, so that individuals don't have to begin all over again each generation. That is, the core of culture is its positive adaptive function. I, too, have called attention to some of the adaptive mechanisms in the culture of poverty—for example, the low aspiration level helps to reduce frustration, the legitimization of short-range hedonism makes possible spontaneity and enjoyment. However, on the whole it seems to me that it is a relatively thin culture. There is a great deal of pathos, suffering and emptiness among those who live in the culture of poverty. It does not provide much support or long-range satisfaction and its encouragement of mistrust tends to magnify helplessness and isolation. Indeed, the poverty of culture is one of the crucial aspects of the culture of poverty.

The concept of the culture of poverty provides a high level of generalization which, hopefully, will unify and explain a number of phenomena viewed as distinctive characteristics of racial, national or regional groups.

For example, matrifocality, a high incidence of consensual unions and a high percentage of households headed by women, which have been thought to be distinctive of Caribbean family organization or of Negro family life in the U.S.A., turn out to be traits of the culture of poverty and are found among diverse peoples in many parts of the world and among peoples who have had no history of slavery.

The concept of a cross-societal subculture of poverty enables us to see that many of the problems we think of as distinctively our own or distinctively Negro problems (or that of any other special racial or ethnic group), also exist in countries where there are no distinct ethnic minority groups. This suggests that the elimination of physical poverty per se may not be enough to eliminate the culture of poverty, which is a whole way of life.

What is the future of the culture of poverty? In considering this question, one must distinguish between those countries in which it represents a relatively small segment of the population and those in which it constitutes a very large one. Obviously the solutions will differ in these two situations. In the United States, the major solution proposed by planners and social workers in dealing with multiple-problem families and the so-called hard core of poverty has been to attempt slowly to raise their level of living and to incorporate them into the middle class. Wherever possible, there has been some reliance upon psychiatric treatment.

In the underdeveloped countries, however, where great masses of people live in the culture of poverty, a social-work solution does not seem feasible. Because of the magnitude of the problem, psychiatrists can hardly begin to cope with it. They have all they can do to care for their own growing middle class. In these countries, the people with a culture of poverty may seek a more revolutionary solution. By creating basic structural changes in society, by redistributing wealth, by organizing the poor and giving them a sense of belonging, of power and of leadership, revolutions frequently succeed in abolishing some of the basic characteristics of the culture of poverty, even when they do not succeed in abolishing poverty itself.

NOTES

[1]There has been relatively little discussion of the culture of poverty concept in the professional journals, however. Two articles deal with the problem in some detail: Elizabeth Herzog, "Some Assumptions About the Poor," *The Social Service Review,* (December 1963): 389–402; Lloyd Ohlin, "Inherited Poverty," Organization for Economic Cooperation and Development (n.d.), Paris.

[2]While the term "subculture of poverty" is technically more accurate, I have used "culture of poverty" as a shorter form.

[3]In a unilineal kinship system, descent is reckoned either through males or through females. When traced exclusively through males it is called patrilineal or agnatic descent; when reckoned exclusively through females it is called matrilineal or uterine descent. In a bilateral or cognatic system, descent is traced through males and females without emphasis on either line.

In a unilineal system, the lineage consists of all the descendants of one ancestor. In a patrilineal system, the lineage is composed of all the descendants through males of one male ancestor. A matrilineage consists of all the descendants through females of one female ancestor. The lineage may thus contain a very large number of generations. If bilateral descent is reckoned, however, the number of generations that can be included in a social unit is limited, since the number of ancestors doubles every generation.

Unilineal descent groups ("lineages" or "clans") are corporate groups, in the sense that the lineage or clan may act as a collectivity: it can take blood vengeance against another descent group, it can hold property, etc. However, the bilateral kin group (the "kindred") can rarely act as a collectivity because it is not a "group" except from the point of view of a particular individual, and, furthermore, has no continuity over time.

In a unilineal system, an individual is assigned to a group by virtue of his birth. In contrast, a person born into a bilateral system usually has a choice of relatives whom he chooses to recognize as "kin" and with whom he wants to associate. This generally leads to a greater diffuseness and fragmentation of ties with relatives over time.

[4]"The Culture of Poverty," in John J. Te Paske and S. N. Fischer, eds., *Explosive Forces in Latin America* (Columbus: Ohio State University Press, 1964), pp. 149–173.

[5]A formal organization designed to provide caste leadership.

[6]It may be that in the slums of Calcutta and Bombay an incipient culture of poverty is developing. It would be highly desirable to do family studies there as a crucial test of the culture-of-poverty hypothesis.

[7]Frantz Fanon, *The Wretched of the Earth* (New York: Grove Press, 1965), p. 103.

The Invisible Jewish Poor

Ann G. Wolfe

A decade ago, America was startled to learn that there were among us 30 million people living below what the government considered the poverty line. It took a man of insight and vision, Michael Harrington, to alert most of us to the fact that we lived in a country in which poverty, in its extreme, existed side by side with affluence.[1] For a reason that is not altogether clear, the Jewish community did not recognize the relevance of this phenomenon to its own people. To be sure, from time to time, we would read about a group of Jews living in extreme poverty, but these groups seemed to be few and far between, and with an occasional exception, did not arouse either passion or anxiety in us. It is difficult to explain why it took so long for us to realize that we too, have our poor—our "others"—a situation which now presents us with a new and urgent challenge.

The April 22, 1971 issue of *Jewish Week,* an Anglo-Jewish publication, has as its lead editorial an item with the caption, "Belated Recognition of a Problem." The editorial states:

Editor's Note: Some of the data in this chapter differ from the more recent figures discussed in the introduction. This essay is presented here because it was the first attempt to determine the extent of Jewish poverty and because it presents a national perspective.

Better late than never is the utmost of enthusiasm earned by the announcement of the Central Conference of American Rabbis (Reform), that its incoming President, Rabbi David Polish of Evanston, Illinois, is proposing a far-reaching program of service to the Jewish poor in America.

It is not merely neglect that the American Jewish poor have suffered. They have been the victims of prejudice and discrimination as well. and they have suffered from these attitudes at the hands of fellow Jews. Lest the Reform rabbis be allotted a disproportionate share of the blame for past error because of their present decision to take action, let it be recorded that the whole of the affluent Jewish community, including even much of the Orthodox establishments, is to blame.

Because the myth that the American Jew has conquered poverty has been generally accepted by the affluent Jewish majority, we do not even have reliable statistics on the extent of Jewish poverty.

The publication carries a news item that quotes from Rabbi Polish, to the effect that thousands of Jewish poor families do not have a place in the Jewish community, and he went on, "we have swept the Jewish poor out of sight and acted as though they didn't exist."

In order to understand the dynamics of the change that characterizes the Jewish community in the United States, a look at our history is illuminating. From the end of the 1900s to the mid-1960s, the Jewish population increased rapidly. In 1880, American Jews numbered less than than 250,000 and represented less than half of 1 percent of the total population. By 1970, the Jewish population had increased 25 times in 90 years, compared to a fourfold increase for the total United States population during the same period. Now, at the beginning of the 1970s, the American Jewish community is the largest concentration of Jews in the world, more than two and a half times the numbers of Jews in Israel, and accounts for half of world Jewry.

Secondly, look at the source of our population growth. The tremendous increase in the number of Jews in the United States was not the result of natural growth, as was true for most of the rest of America, but rather it was due to the heavy migration of Eastern European Jews between 1890 and 1924.

Before the 1870s, the American Jewish community was composed largely of first and second generation German Jews who had come to these shores between 1820 and 1870, with the remainder—some of Sephardic origin—descendants of the original Spanish and Portuguese settlers of the colonial period. There were smaller groups from central Europe who were descendants of a pre-nineteenth-century migration. As a result, the striking feature that defines the character of the American Jewish community evolved out of the Jewish immigration from Eastern Europe at the turn of the century. However, the character of the American Jewish community is now changing, as a result of internal forces at work among native-born American Jews. The transition from a foreign-born, immigrant group to an Americanized second and third generation community has important consequences for the structure of the Jewish community, and for the ways in which American Jews live. For the first time in the history of the American Jewish community, a third generation Jewish population is facing the American scene without large-scale outside reinforcement. We are now on our own, so to speak. It is this fact that sets up the framework for an understanding of the phenomenon of our Jewish poor, and the invisible character of Jewish poverty.

Another significant historical fact should be noted. In his study of the social and religious history of the Jew, Salo Baron observed that as early as the mid-seventeenth century, it was already noticeable that "great destructive forces, contagious diseases, and wars, seem to have claimed fewer victims among the Jews than among their gentile neighbors." Whether the health and mortality differentials noted by Baron for the mid-seventeenth century also characterize the American Jewish community today, has not been fully explored. However, what little data is available indicates that some differences do exist between the survival pattern of Jews and that of the total white population. There appear to be lower death rates of Jews at younger ages. The lower Jewish birth rate has resulted in a Jewish population today with an unusually large number of elderly persons: one out of every ten Jews is over the age of 65.

We have no up-to-date scientific data on many of the characteristics of the Jewish population in America. We have pieces of information on income, occupation, age distribution, education, etc. Studies done at different times, in different cities; surveys of special functional agencies, census reports—these help us put together the pieces of the puzzle. Hopefully, more accurate information will be forthcoming from the national population study currently being conducted by the Council of Jewish Federations and Welfare Funds (CJFWF).

Age is an important, basic demographic feature. At the present time, and until the national population study of the CJFWF is completed, the only national information on the age composition of the Jewish community is the 1957 census survey: Changes have undoubtedly occurred since then. However, the data clearly indicates that the Jewish population is, on the whole, older than that of the general white population of the United States. The youngest age group, under 14, make up 23 percent of the total Jewish population, compared to 28 percent of the total white population. Also according to the 1957 census, 28 percent of U. S. Jews are in the age range of 45 to 64, as opposed to 21 percent of the total U. S. white population. We can expect therefore, that the proportion of older people in the Jewish population will continue to increase during the next decade.

In American society, the problems associated with an

aged population are serious. During the next few decades, such problems may be even more serious for the Jewish community than for the population as a whole. The proportion of persons within the Jewish population who are 65 years of age and over, is expected to increase from 10 percent, at the present time, to 17 percent in 1978.

Overall, therefore, it would seem that the Jewish age structure requires continuous assessing, not only for its impact on births, deaths and the economic structure of the community, but also because of its broader sociological implications, and because of the need to plan services for the future. In an as yet unpublished demographic profile of the American Jew conducted for the American Jewish Community,[2] Dr. Sidney Goldstein of the department of sociology at Brown University states:

> While recognizing that the general trend is toward an aging population, with its associated problems of housing, financial crises resulting from retirement, more illness, one must also be aware that changes are taking place at other points in the age hierarchy and that the needs for schools, playgrounds, camps, and teenage programs, also vary as the age profile changes. Too often, the Jewish community has been guilty of planning its future without taking account of the basic considerations of the probable size distribution and age composition of the population.

The past decade has brought increasing technological advances, leaving behind institutions and people who have become both out of fashion and ill-equipped to deal with our society's changing needs. Some of us believe that many of our most serious national problems stem from the failure of our institutions to adapt to change. In the Jewish community, we see a larger aging population unable to adapt to a new and different society and, if we are candid, the same failure of national institutions to take cognizance of these changes.

Part of the blame lies with the institutions, but the greater portion of the blame lies with us. For more than a decade after World War II, until the 1960s began to shake us out of our complacency, many of us were content to sit back and take comfort in the fact that we had never had it so good. It was during this period that we, and the country as a whole, became convinced of the affluence of the entire Jewish community; this often created problems for us. All the statistical figures on income showed the Jewish community enjoying higher average incomes and higher median income than that of the general population. The researcher encounters the greatest difficulty in collecting information on the income of Americans. Not until 1940 did the federal census include a question on this topic. Of the larger number of Jewish community surveys, very few collected information on income, and some of the information which was collected is often questionable. However, a small number of national surveys did include such questions, and these clearly demonstrated that the income level of Jews is above that of the general population. A study conducted at the University of Michigan more than ten years ago[3] indicated that 31 percent of Jewish families had incomes of $7,500 to $15,000, compared to only 16 percent of the general population. The National Opinion Research Survey made at about the same time collected similar data.[4] The median income for heads of Jewish households was just under $6,000, compared to just over $4,000 for the total population. Somehow, these facts were deceptive; they hid others, that were less impressive.

It is in these studies that we first find significant indications of the extent of poverty within the Jewish community. The National Opinion Research Survey on income related to religion, reported that 15.3 percent of

Jewish households, 15.6 percent of Catholics, and 22.7 percent of Protestants had incomes under $3,000 a year.[5]

Who are the Jewish poor? Who are those in the Jewish community who have not made it, who are not making it, and who live their lives in quiet desperation, out of the mainstream of the Jewish community?

We have many blind spots in our vision, particularly when we try to look at ourselves. An interesting example of a blind spot relates to "wealthy" Miami Beach. In a study done in Miami's South Beach area,[6] it was learned that 40,000 people were clustered in an area of some 30 square blocks. Of these, 80 percent are over 65, and 85 percent are Jews. The average annual income is $2,460; thus thousands are living on less than $28.00 a week for rent and food.

Elderly Jews, the remnants of the vast immigration of the early twentieth century, constitute the largest group of Jews living in poverty. In spite of all the figures I have given, we do not know precisely what proportion of the poor in our community is elderly. The eight or nine community studies which we have reviewed reveal that something like 60 to 65 percent of Jews living in poverty are over 60 or 65 years of age. An impressionistic look at the needs of the elderly poor discloses that the major problem facing the elderly poor is housing. Their living conditions are often inadequate, with homes in various stages of dilapidation or disrepair. Frequently, they need help in improving their current housing, or assistance in relocating. They often find themselves the last holdouts in areas that have ceased being Jewish. Loneliness and isolation are perhaps the most poignant characteristics of old age, and these are reinforced for the Jewish elderly who are locked into neighborhoods that no longer offer them the support and security they need. More significant than emotional insecurity is the sense of physical fright that the deteriorating neighborhood induces.

The aged often live alone (two out of three, according to one report), as widows or widowers, in housing arrangements that do not allow for much meaningful social contact with others. In the survey of the Miami Beach area to which I referred earlier, the people need financial help. They need to be able to pay the skyrocketing rents and have some money left over from their Social Security checks so that they can eat adequately. In addition to this they ask for simple things. Some said the best thing would would be to get a hot lunch in a congenial setting where they could meet others and spend a few pleasant hours. Some of the people who were interviewed said they would like to have group activities that were not, as one man put it, "children's games for old people." One man who was interviewed said, rather matter-of-factly, that he had come to Miami Beach for a "warm death bed," and now found himself on a picket line protesting the increasing rents in the area.

An unpublished study conducted in Los Angeles revealed that there are about 8,000 elderly Jews receiving public assistance there, and that a much larger number would be eligible who did not apply, for a variety of reasons: pride, lack of knowledge of what is available, physical inability to get to the welfare office. Over 18,000 indigent elderly Jews live in households with incomes below $4,000 a year.

We owe a great debt to the present population of the elderly in our community, because they were the ones who helped build it. The vast numbers managed on their own—some had some help, but for the most part they were a vigorous, powerful, independent force. It should be possible for them to live out their years involved in life and cared for, and we should make it clear by what we do that we value their lives, their experience, the work of their hands, their humor, and their constant hope.

In a recently published book about the elderly Jews in an

old age home,[7] this hope is expressed clearly by one resident
of the home who said:

> I don't want to talk about the past . . . I don't want to think I
> am getting older. I want to think about living. Now the world
> is altogether different. I like to know about the future. I want
> to look through a window to see how it will be after I am gone.
> I want to know about this world.

The aged who make up about two thirds of our poor
are perhaps easier to see, and evoke sentiments that all of us
feel. But there are significant numbers of poor who are
not old folks, and I think it is important to explode the
myth that all the Jewish poor are also old.

There is less sympathy for this other segment—30–35
percent of our poverty group—which is made up of single,
unrelated people or families, many with young children,
some headed by one parent. There are Jewish families
receiving Aid to Dependent Children, a fact that is usually
greeted with disbelief. In New York City alone it is estimated
that one quarter of a million Jews subsist on less than
$3,500 a year, and another 150,000 live at near-poverty
level, on incomes below $4,500. A study undertaken in
1963–64 by the Columbia University School of Public
Health and Administrative Medicine,[8] shows that 10 percent of the Jewish population is sustaining itself on $3,000 a
year or less. For the foreign-born Jews in New York City,
this figure rises to 15.7 percent, fairly similar to the Puerto
Rican community where 16.3 percent are living on under
$3,000 a year. 75 percent of the foreign-born Jews in
New York are 50 years of age and older, but in addition to
this aging population, there are Orthodox and Hasidic
poor, many of them with young families. There are 80,000
Hasidic Jews in New York City, and this group is the
third largest poverty group in New York.

Philadelphia, a study conducted by the Jewish Employment and Vocational Service of that city,[9] reveals what

some of us have long suspected—that we are like everybody else. Unemployed Jews who came to this agency have the same problems that the poor members of any group have. The study covered a sample of Jewish men and women representing an active caseload of more than 700 persons. The age range was from 17 to over 65 years, and about half of them were in their prime work period, between the ages of 21 and 50. One third of the persons coming for help with employment had had incomes during the previous year of less than $2,600, and one in six had had an annual income of $4,000 or more.

Up until the very recent past, we have had a long period of full employment in America. Thus, jobless persons have usually been people with severe problems of a personal nature, or those against whom society discriminated. In the Philadelphia study, it appeared that six out of ten of the Jews coming for help with employment had disabilities classified as primarily emotional, but this group overlapped with another group of four out of ten who had problems relating to aging or physical health. Limited education was found to be an important factor among poor Jews, half of the job seekers having less than 11 years of schooling, and one in five with less than an eighth grade education. Here, too, our blind spots operate. Because of the high proportion of young Jews in college today, and our tradition as the "People of the Book," we tend to overlook the earlier generation that has had a less impressive education.

In commenting on this study the Executive Director said:

> The conditions of impoverishment in spirit as well as economically, which is typical, and the social dependency among other minority groups which stems from exclusion, rejection and chronic failure are operative in the Jewish population as well.
>
> · · · ·
>
> It seems apparent that—in the case of Jewish Employment Vocational Service clients, at least, vocational handicaps underlie their separation from the mainstream of the self-respecting, self-supporting members of society.

One might consider too, current situations of economic recession and rising unemployment, and its effect on that part of the Jewish community which lives marginally.

In summarizing the problem of the Jewish poor—estimated at 700,000 to 800,000 in the United States—we must state that their problems are common to all poor people, but that there are problems peculiar to Jews, problems in intergroup relations, problems related to a Jewish identity which exist in a society whose image of the Jew is not altogether accurate, an image which the Jewish community persists in perpetuating. These problems include poor housing, inadequate medical care, neighborhoods that are undesirable in terms of emotional and physical security, since they are outside the Jewish cultural mainstream.

There are special needs in the Orthodox community to which we must pay particular attention. There are demands which Jewish ritual makes—the need to buy kosher food, for example. The Hasidic community has a built-in resistance to secular education, particularly at the high school and college levels. Few Hasidim have a college degree, an impediment to benefiting from the economic advantages which higher education normally brings. Jewish education for this group drains the resources of the Hasidic family. On religious grounds, the Orthodox and Hasidic communities are opposed to birth control and tend to have large families. In Williamsburg, in New York City, the median family size is 6.3 children, as opposed to the average Jewish family size of 2 children.

I am making a plea to "raise our consciousness"—a phrase borrowed from Women's Liberation. What, then, is to be done and who is to do it?

Future historians are likely to see the pattern of Jewish community organization as the unique characteristic of twentieth-century Jewry. It has become a model for the structure of voluntary organizations of other religious and ethnic groups. Students from all corners of the globe come to study the complex of Jewish health, welfare, and other agencies. We have the structure and the processes for rational planning. What we must now do in my opinion, is to use our structures in a way that is more responsive to the needs which we now perceive. And in moving towards this responsiveness, I suggest that some basic questions be asked:

—Who decides what service gets how much money?
—What process is used in making this decision?
—Do all the elements in the Jewish community share in this decision-making process?
—How are priorities set? Where is the power?
—Does the Jewish community need to re-order its domestic priorities?
—Are we paying enough attention to our domestic Jewish needs?

In the process of finding answers to these and related questions, we may renew the spirit which motivated the formation of Jewish services during the early years, the underlying belief that we must care for each other and that the suffering and pain of any in our community affects us all.

NOTES

[1]Michael Harrington, *The Other America; Poverty in the United States,* (Baltimore: Penguin Books, 1963).

[2]Sidney Goldstein, "American Jewry 1970: A Demographic Profile?" *1971 American Jewish Year Book*, Volume 72, pp. 3–88.

[3]Bernard Lazerwitz, "Family Income by Religious Group," *Journal of American Statistical Association* (September, 1961).

[4]*Distribution of Income by Religious Groups*—1962, National Opinion Research Center, University of Chicago, Illinois.

[5]Ibid.

[6]*Socio-Economic Study of the South Shore of Miami Beach, Florida,* Welfare Planning Council of Dade County, Florida, November, 1968.

[7]Dorothy Rabinowitz and Yedida Nielsen, *Home Life* (New York: Macmillan, 1971).

[8]J. Elinson, D. W. Haberman, C. Gell, *Ethnic and Educational Data on Adults in New York City* 1963–64 (New York: School of Public Health and Administrative Medicine, Columbia University, 1967).

[9]Saul S. Leshner, "Poverty in the Jewish Community", *Journal of Jewish Communal Service* Vol. 53, No. 3 (Spring 1967): 245.

Jews Without Money, Revisited
Paul Cowan

The poverty among the poor Jews who live on New
York's Lower East Side compares to poverty I've seen
anywhere in America—in Mississippi, the South Bronx,
East Los Angeles. Most people think of the Jewish immigration as the most spectacularly successful one in
American history, but the 50-year journey from the
shtetle to the Space Age left many casualties in its wake.
An estimated 250,000 Jews in New York City live below
the poverty level of $3500; an estimated 150,000 more
earn less than $4500 a year. Most of them are over 65, and
many are Orthodox, but there are young people among
them, too, and Jews with all shades of religious belief.
They live all over New York City: in Far Rockaway, in
Coney Island, for example, in Borough Park, and on the
Upper West Side. I interviewed scores who still live on the
Lower East Side.

There is a myth that this area, once the portal for the
large, energetic Eastern European Jewish immigration,
has changed completely: that blacks and Puerto Ricans
dominate the neighborhood, while all the Jews who used to
live there have moved to Borough Park, Forest Hills,
the Upper West Side or Scarsdale. But a 1971 Human
Resources Administration report showed that 62 percent
of the neighborhood's population was white, 24 percent
was Puerto Rican and 14 percent was black. About 10,000

39

"Jews without money," in a phrase Michael Gold's book made popular nearly 50 years ago, still live there.

Traces of the earlier era remain. North of Delancey, Rivington Street and Orchard Street are still noisy, open-air markets, where Yiddish-speaking, yarmulke-wearing Jews inveigle virtually every passerby to purchase their cut-rate shoes or pants, their briny pickles or strong-smelling fish. Only now most of their customers are Puerto Ricans, not Jews from Eastern Europe's shtetls, and most of the Jews who own the small stores and the warehouses that line the quieter streets near East Broadway have earned enough money to move outside the neighborhood. So the market is no longer an old world bazaar, where landsman haggles with landsman in terms that are familiar to everyone involved. And though the relations between the shopkeepers and their customers are usually quite friendly, there are occasional unsettling signs of the tensions that plague the neighborhood. At lunchtime one day a drunken black man walked down the street yelling "Jew bastard" at merchant after merchant—an unusual exception to the rule of civility, but one which echoes menacingly in the memories of Jews who have endured pogroms or concentration camps. In one warehouse, a city inspector searched for the owner to tell him that his application for a gun permit had been granted.

Walk into the courtyard of the city-owned Vladeck Houses, near the Henry Street Settlement House, just a few blocks from the corner of East Broadway and Rutgers, which the Daily Forward building, the Garden Cafeteria and Seward Park once made the hub of immigrant life. When the project was built more than 30 years ago, the bulk of its population was Jewish. Many of those people moved away. Now it houses mainly Puerto Ricans and blacks. But on a hot summer day you can still see plenty of old Jews sunning themselves on the benches of the noisy courtyard. For them, the immigrant days are faint, irrelevant memories. Most of them would rather grieve than reminisce.

Many live on social security checks and small pensions, often averaging less than $200 a month income. One reason they stay in the project is that the rents there are so low—about $35 a month. They're too proud to supplement that income by applying for welfare. (Many of them still call welfare by its 1930s name, "relief," and complain that it subsidizes black and Puerto Rican crime). They are afflicted with the diseases of the aged—diabetes, arthritis, Parkinson's disease. Many are widows or widowers, haunted by memories of dead relatives. And they are terrified of muggers and thieves.

They feel as if they've been abandoned by uptown liberal Jewish intellectuals, politicians and philanthropists who, they think, care more about blacks and Puerto Ricans than about the nagging problems of the Jewish slums. And, worse than that, they have been abandoned by their own children. Many successful young people who have escaped the neighborhood haven't sent their parents money or even mail in years. And many of those who still help out do so with visible annoyance. It is impossible to know the inner history of each family situation—whether a particular parent was unforgivably cruel to his offspring, or whether a particular child is now unforgivably insensitive to his parent—but it's clear that now many old people on the Lower East Side feel a lasting bitterness toward assimilated, middle-class Jews—their children. Some were secretly happy about the problems that afflicted them in Forest Hills. "They've never helped us out," one old man in the Vladeck Projects told me. "Why should we care about them. They got what they deserved."

During my weeks on the Lower East Side I began to feel some ethnic loyalties I never knew I possessed. Yet I also realized that, in real life, I represented many of the things the people I met there were complaining about.

I have always lived in an assimilated environment. I married a gentile without feeling a trace of emotional conflict. I knew very little about my religious heritage. During the past decade I've worked with blacks in the civil rights movement and Latins in the Peace Corps but, except for a six-month stay in Israel, I have never worked with or written about dispossessed Jews—or even realized that they existed in America.

I've always seen my politics as an outgrowth of the Jewish tradition that obliged one to work with the oppressed, both because it was morally right and because the oppression of a group like the blacks could quickly spread out to include the Jews. These are still my deep commitments, of course, but as I grew to care about people on the Lower East Side I became intensely aware that many of them would regard my ideas and activities as a form of betrayal. And the more I learned about their problems the more unsettling that contradiction became. One morning I visited a man I'll call Moishe Kimmel, an 87-year-old former watchmaker—"Moishe the cleanly," as he calls himself proudly. He came over here from Warsaw 60 years ago, after a series of episodes in which Polish soldiers beat him up because he was a Jew and happened to be walking the streets after curfew.

Moishe found a job in a Lower East Side shop and learned English fast enough to skip quickly over the "greenhorn" phase every immigrant dreaded. Now he speaks with only the pleasant trace of an accent. But during the Depression his wife died, and the small store were he worked went bankrupt. He had a nervous breakdown and was hospitalized for several years. When he got out, a settlement house gave him a job greeting visitors. He kept a very careful guest book, and told everyone that celebrities like Mrs. Roosevelt and Herbert Lehman who met him on brief visits were his very close friends.

Now he is too old to stray far from his three-room

apartment in the Vladeck Project. He must be terribly lonely. One day I met him in the project courtyard and he invited me to visit him at home. When I came to his apartment several days later, he kissed my cheek with joy. He's a short, frail man whose constant, eager grin makes it impossible to believe he has serious problems. He had to stand on tiptoes to reach my face with his lips.

Then, proudly, he showed me around his immaculate apartment. The brown frame house, with windows and green shutters, that he had built out of popsicle sticks and cellophane. "I'm a genius with my hands," he said. The shrine he'd built around a routine letter from Herbert Lehman, thanking him for some shred of political advice. The police whistle and bogus badge he'd gotten, as a favor, from some friendly cop at the Seventh Precinct Station. The clean ties and perfectly pressed suits that filled about a third of one small closet. The spotless, empty refrigerator. The galoshes he polished last March to make sure they'd stay in shape for the next winter. "This is the cleanest of all the 3071 apartments here," Moishe told me joyfully.

Until a few years ago he used to go out at night to sit in a small park in Water Street, where his compulsive gregariousness could find an outlet in conversations with old friends. Then, about 18 months ago, he was mugged in the lobby of his building. The muggers got 30 cents. It happened again a few weeks ago, when he was walking to the Gouverneur Clinic for a check-up. Two black men darted out of a cluster of bushes, shoved him hard enough that he fell to the ground, and ripped his pocket from his shirt, where they found a dollar. Moishe rarely goes out any more. He's quite bitter about blacks and Latins. "Maybe some of them are good—about 10 percent. But you have to look for them. I don't trust any of them any more, even the nice ones. I wouldn't let them into my apartment."

After the first mugging Moishe's daughter, the wife of a successful doctor, offered to rent him a small apartment a few blocks away from her house in Yonkers. But she never mentioned the suggestion again. "It's all right," he says. "I never wanted to go there anyway. I ask her all the time how come she doesn't keep kosher, and she always argues back. And her house. It's such a mess." But she does visit him occasionally. She was coming later that afternoon, to leave her cat with Moishe while she and her husband and kids went off on a short vacation. He was very excited about the prospect of a weekend companion. Before I left he showed me the tidy corner of the living room where he'd placed a pillow from his bed for the cat to sleep on, and asked if a smart fellow like me had any ideas about how I could make it cozier.

Many old Jews like Moishe genuinely prefer the threatening streets of the Lower East Side to the half-goyishe suburbs where their assimilated children live. They know where to find glat kosher butchers, stores that observe the proper Sabbath, Orthodox shuls that preserve the traditions they learned as children. Modern Americanized neighborhoods leave them depressed and disoriented.

Yet most of the institutions that give the neighborhood its special character are now under siege. Take the synogogue. Even now, in the Lower East Side's decline, there are still 52 functioning shuls, many of which were founded a half-century ago by landsmen from small villages in Russia or Poland, who wanted to preserve their special local traditions. Now several synagogues have to share the same rabbi and many rabbis have to find secular jobs to supplement their incomes.

Each morning and night, frail old men forge the daily link to their childhood faith, davening, gossiping in the tiny, musty attic and celllike shuls, most of which are clustered onto a two-block area on East Broadway. The synagogues aren't only houses of worship—they're centers of study and homes for the lonely, whose chatter forms a noisy counterpoint to each evening's services. Now, though, the congregants of shuls that once thrived often find it impossible to gather a minyan (the 10 men necessary to recite the Kaddish, the prayers for the dead), because some last surviving members are too ill to walk the few blocks to the place of worship.

Or as frequently happens, they are too frightened of crime. Many synagogues in the area have been vandalized or burned. Their windows are frequently broken. One of the neighborhood's oldest yeshivas, Rabbi Jacob Joseph, is moving uptown. One reason is that the building is old and decaying, but another is that many children and their parents were frightened for their personal safety. Many shuls have had to compromise with Jewish tradition and hold ma'ariv, evening prayer, before sundown so the congregants can walk home in the waning daylight.

One night I went to a small basement shul near the Forward building on East Broadway with a man in his early sixties, a cab driver who had only become religious as he realized that death was approaching. I was always uncomfortable going to these synagogues. I kept worrying that some elderly Orthodox man would realize I didn't know the rituals, and wheel at me and denounce me as an imposter. So I'd rock back and forth a little, faking a daven; I'd try to remember to turn the prayer book's pages backward, following the Hebrew text; I'd mutter a few moaning sounds hoping that whoever heard me would hear my barely audible creaks as the appropriate prayer.

It was the week of Tishah B'Av, the anniversary of the destruction of the first and second temples in Jerusalem, a period of mourning for all Orthodox Jews. The bimah, the pulpit, was shrouded with black curtains, and only a few candles lit the murky room. The congregants chanted dirges from the Book of Lamentations. There was a fervor to the ceremony that left me unexpectedly moved, though I could only understand the tiniest portion of what was going on. Yet there was something ghostly about the fervor. The shul, the ceremony, belonged to the aged: I was the only person there under 60.

After the service the cab driver made a point of waiting for two other congregants, bearded men in their eighties wearing the caftans and wide hats of the very Orthodox. They walked very slowly, hobbling on canes. He was careful to remain a few paces behind them. It seemed to be a nightly routine, an attempt at protection. As we passed a group of Puerto Rican teenagers, talking rapid Spanish, I could see him grow tense and watchful. "Sometimes they harass the old ones. They knock off their hats or call them ugly names. It's not only them. I remember the days when the Italians and the Irish did the same thing to us. But it didn't happen so often in our own neighborhood then. At least in those days we knew that these few blocks belonged to us."

As much as they can, the elderly Jews who are dispersed in the Lower East Side's projects and tenements try to provide mutal comfort. (For the most part they don't seem to have much contact with the younger, more affluent Jews who have moved into the middle-income cooperative developments that have been built in the neighborhood during the past 10 years.)

The owner of a tiny basement grocery store on Rivington Street, the survivor of a concentration camp in Russia, slips a few extra rolls each day to a senile old widow who ravages the block's wastebaskets for food, who never bathes or changes her single, tattered dress, who lives in pitch darkness because she can't afford to pay her tenement electric bills. I stood in the store one morning and watched his wife pose delicate questions to each customer who came in, extracting their psychic news. (How thriftily they examined each piece of cheese, each loaf of bread as they talked, as if the decision to spend 50 cents on food was

the most crucial one of their day.) She uses the store as a
mental health listening post, and tells Lisa Schwab of the
Gouverneur Mobile Crisis Unit if anyone seems on the
brink of a breakdown.

After shul one night I watched a stooped, half-blind
old man while he bought some tomatoes at a small fruit
stand. He paid $1; he received $1.25 worth of goods. The
transaction was so familiar to the customer and the
shopkeeper, so laden with unspoken pride and shame and
trust, that the storeowner chided me angrily when I
mentioned his generosity. Later that evening I ate a dairy
supper at the Garden Cafeteria (where a $2 dinner is a once-
a-year luxury for thousands of people like Moishe Kimmel).
I sat with a retired tailor, born in Poland, who had just
returned from Israel after his host, a cousin who'd invited
him for a visit after a 40-year separation, had died one night
when they were sleeping in the same bed. The man was eager
to get home to watch Carol Burnett. He lived alone, and his
greatest pleasure was watching comedies on TV. But he
made a point of waiting until 8:15, 15 minutes after the
show began, so he could buy a fresh copy of the Daily
Forward from an old Jew who peddled the paper at the
Garden Delicatessen, who needed every piece of business
he could get to pay his $45 rent.

On shabbos morning the entire community comes alive.
Then, the shuls on East Broadway are filled with men and
boys wearing their prayer shawls, chanting, singing
Hebrew songs like "Erov Ha Shoshanim," which echo up
and down the block. In some, smaller groups cluster
around spare wooden tables savoring long discussions
of complex passages from the Talmud, discussions which
have been raging for centuries. The walk back to the
projects can be like a stroll through the streets of the
shtetl. The men and boys stop each other on their way home,
wish each other a good shabbos, dwell together for several
minutes chatting in English and Yiddish. For those few

hours the streets really do belong to the Orthodox. And even in the projects you can glimpse very old people, too frail to go to shul, visiting each other at mealtime, spending an afternoon together where the tide of rich memory washes away the present's loneliness and fear.

But the fabric of mutual support is thin. It usually dissolves when the outside world becomes a menacing presence. Then ancient fears recur and become oppressive. The lack of needed community institutions is then clear.

The Good Companion Club, which is sponsored by the Henry Street Settlement House, is an organization for people over 65, whose headquarters is in the basement of one building in the Vladeck Project. It features a lunch program, where about 300 people, including about 45 who are homebound, receive nourishing meals for about 60 cents a day. After lunch one day a woman came into the club yelling that a lady who lived in a nearby courtyard had just been robbed. I went over to her apartment to check out the story. Since the victim spoke only Yiddish, I had to ask a Jewish woman in the courtyard out front to translate for me.

When my interpreter first heard what had happened she began to wail sympathetically: "Such a nice lady. She came over from Russia 40 years ago, and she's never hurt anybody." But as she listened to the details, relaying them to me, she got angrier and angrier at the victim. The woman had apparently been chosen because she'd taken $16 from her purse and counted it on the street. The translator was livid: "Sixteen years in this project, and she doesn't even know enough to leave her pocketbook at home. She thinks she's living on Park Avenue? This is a jungle. Listen," she said, still in English, turning to the woman and grabbing her arm, "when you go out from now on you put your money here." And she thrust her hand between the woman's breasts. "That's the only way you can be at all sure of being safe."

It was about half an hour after the robbery. By then the victim had begun to wonder what I, a strange man, was doing, calmly taking notes about her plight. When the interpreter explained that I was a newspaper reporter, she began to cry even more loudly than she had when she talked about the crime. "She doesn't want her name in the newspaper," the translator says. "She's afraid maybe her daughter will see it. Maybe she'll get so aggravated she won't send checks any more."

I was familiar with that request. At least half the old people I interviewed asked for anonymity in order to ward off some offspring's rage. So I said I'd describe the episode, but disguise some details and change her name, as I have in other incidents.

Then the translator got nervous. "You're not going to mention my name are you?" (I didn't even know it). "How can that help me? You can see that we're surrounded here." She gestured toward the courtyard, the neighboring apartments. "Who knows what they can do to us. We don't even want them to know our names, or what we think. We just say, hi, how are you, we're as polite as can be. That's our only chance of being left in peace.

Many of the people I spoke to at the Vladeck Houses told me that when the place first opened, more than 30 years ago, the Jews, who filled most of the apartments, regarded the place as a paradise in comparison with the cramped, rat-filled tenements where they'd spent their earliest years in America.

Now, add to their isolation and their fear of crime the fact that the city often provides the projects with services that are nearly as flawed as were the services in the tenements. There are only a few guards for the entire area, which stretches across several city blocks. As a moneysaving device, the city installed elevators that stop on every other floor, which means that heart patients, or arthritics, or people with Parkinson's disease, who live on odd floors must hobble down a flight of stairs in order to get home. The unprotected stairways, of course, are attractive turf for muggers. The elevator, which smells of urine, is only cleaned every several days. Frequently the lights in the elevators are broken, which means that people don't go up to their apartments until they can find trusted friends to accompany them. (The door to each building is double-locked, though. You can't enter by a buzzer system, but only if someone inside lets you in with a key. People who live in the project say that this precaution, which began after a rash of murders in the nearby Baruch Houses last year, has reduced the amount of mugging.) On the day I talked with the woman who'd been robbed, the elevator in a nearby building was broken altogether. I knew because when I passed through that courtyard, on my way to get a cup of coffee at the Garden Cafeteria, a swarm of old Jews mistook me for an elevator man. It was about 2:30 in the afternoon. They complained that the elevator had been broken since 9 AM. They'd missed meals, doses of medicine, naps. Some were worried that they'd been in the sun too long to suit their doctors' orders.

In an abandoned community like the Lower East Side, most people want desperately to believe that an outsider with a smile and a moment to listen, is the representative of some mysterious, benign power that will somehow help them. I explained that I was a reporter, not a mechanic, but that didn't do any good. I was also a novelty: someone who'd at least listen to sorrows that the neighbors had heard to the point of boredom, who at best might bring relief. One woman, using the broken elevator as a pretext, reached into the sack under her stocking where she kept her treasured belongings and showed me the heart pills she took twice a day, and then the special ones she was supposed to put under her tongue in case of an attack. Did I think the doctors had given her the right prescription? And an old man removed his dentures, showed me a deep chip where his molars should be, and asked if I knew whether his Medicaid would provide for a new set of teeth.

A man in his early seventies stopped to talk to me on his way to work. He had diverticulitis, he said, and painful arthritis in his hands. But he couldn't afford to live on social security alone. "I didn't want to go on relief, though, like the colored do. That's the trouble with this neighborhood. The government is paying for those people so they don't have to work, and they can spend their days mugging us. I'm different from them. I don't want to take anyone's handouts. So I got a job as a messenger. I work four hours a day, and I earn enough money to pay for what I want."

A 73-year-old widow with crippling arthritis, whom I'll call Sylvia Goldstein, was sitting on one of the courtyard benches and she called me over to her. I'd met her several days earlier with one of the Good Companion social workers. He'd taken me to her dark, crowded, three-room apartment because her bleak situation seemed typical of the way hundreds of people in the neighborhood were living.

Her 70-year-old brother and his wife, both victims of Parkinson's disease, lived in the front room. It was early afternoon when we entered, but the shades were drawn. They were lying down on separate beds. I could see their hands pushing upward against their white sheets, trembling uncontrollably. The man, once a clothes fitter, had had the disease for 20 years and is completely bedridden. His wife, who only got it three years ago, can still move around the house. She got out of bed the afternoon I was there to talk to the social worker about some pills. Her whole body shook when she stood. Her voice was a faint sound out of a distorting echo chamber. She could barely see or hear.

Sylvia has been trying to get the two of them into an old age home. But she hasn't found any that will allow the man and woman to live together. The couple is childless.

They've been married for 50 years. They refuse to sign any papers that might let some unknown, malevolent bureaucrat separate them. So Sylvia keeps them in with her, defying a city regulation which limits the number of tenants who can live in a three-room apartment. She is constantly terrified that her transgression will be discovered and she'll be evicted. That was one reason she insisted I disguise her name.

She also lives with a middle-aged daughter, a woman who has been suffering from deep depression that prevents her from holding a job. When I came in the daughter was still in her nightclothes, looking quite disheveled. Sylvia says she's like that every day, that she's sought psychiatric assistance but that it hasn't helped her. One of Sylvia's granddaughters also lives in the apartment, though she was visiting relatives in Brooklyn the day I was there. Since her husband, a housepainter, left her a year ago, she's usually been bedridden with migraine headaches. Her son, who's three, has no one to play with. He hasn't yet learned to talk. The social worker told me that once when he came into the apartment the kid was standing in the kind of crib children usually quit using at the age of two, urine dripping down his leg, crying loudly. But Sylvia was too weak to lift him out of the crib, and the other two women couldn't get themselves together enough to help. One wonders about this child's future.

Sylvia is too proud to apply for welfare—no social worker can persuade her that the money is a right, not a gift. The entire family lives on social security checks, Sylvia's and her brother's, and on a monthly pension check of $17 that Sylvia receives from the citywide restaurant chain where she waitressed for 25 years. (Until this year, that check was for $84 a month but Sylvia showed me a form letter she'd received from the president of the company explaining that because of the recession it would have to be cut drastically. She didn't want me to name the company for fear that some diligent bureaucrat would discover she had complained to the press, learn the real name behind my disguise, and cut her off the pension rolls altogether.)

Sylvia talks about her afflictions with a surprising sprightliness. It occurred to me that her ability to survive them with good humor, like Moishe Kimmel's ability to keep his apartment immaculate, might represent a last precious proof that she still has the internal resources to defeat death. Her brave smiles might be her subtle way of raging against the dying of the light.

At noon every day she likes to leave her apartment and hobble over to the basement headquarters of the Good Companion Club. (She's been going there for years, but she never told the staff about the brother and sister-in-law in her apartment, for fear that word of their presence would spread to the building authorities. Recently, though, a friend told a Good Companion worker about the couple. It took weeks to persuade Sylvia that the entire family wouldn't be evicted if they received food at home.)

She's grateful for the Good Companion meals—she couldn't afford such solid, nourishing fare on her own. But the thing she cares about most is the free bingo game the club conducts after lunch every day. That was what she wanted to talk to me about. She likes the relieving excitement of the game, of course. But the excitement is particularly intense because of the chance that, with each game, she might win the prize, an orange, which is a real, cherished delicacy to her.

The first time I visited her I told her I'd be her partner one day and give her the orange if I won it. I made the comment as a half-joking conversation piece. She took it as a firm commitment.

And she hollered at me in the courtyard to complain that she hadn't seen me since then. Had I forgotten her? There was a little laughter in her voice, but the angry reproachful tone that lay just beneath it startled me. I had to promise to join her the next day.

I couldn't get out of that courtyard. Everybody wanted to tell me a tale, to seek my advice. An unusally vivacious old woman told me how she planned to go on an outing to Lancaster County, Pennsylvania, that Saturday with a group from the Henry Street Settlement House. "I'll be the only white person," she laughed, "a regular lily of the valley." She was a widow who lived on her $140 social security check each month, and though her rent was low and her usual diet sparse (a few pieces of American cheese, a hard-boiled egg, some tuna fish, and rice every day), the $11 Henry Street was charging meant quite a chunk out of her budget. The cost seemed particularly high to me since her strict observance of kosher laws would force her to forego the sumptuous Pennsylvania Dutch meal the other travelers would enjoy. She planned to nibble at a cheese sandwich she would pack herself.

The trip was worth it, though. She'd gone last year, and had been awed by the beauty of the countryside. It was the first time she'd been out of New York since she came here 65 years ago, as a six-year-old child. But the money. . . she'd been too proud to apply for welfare, but now she was thinking of asking for food stamps. "They'd be such a help. But I keep worrying they'd degrade me. I know I'm a stubborn old woman. What do you think?"

I said I thought she should take whatever help she could get, but before we could continue talking an old man, whose breath smelled like stale cheese, started tugging at my shirt and talking at me, in heavily accented English, about some obscure fight between him and some old friend about how much money he'd paid for his daughter's wedding. I gathered I was supposed to be the referee. "Shut up, Bernie," said a woman who'd just joined the cluster of people around me. "Everybody knows your story." Then, out-screaming him, she described how she'd almost fainted crossing Grand Street a few days ago. Did I know whether Medicare could help her get a free cane?

I was beginning to feel a little hysterical when an old pudgy woman I'll call Rebecca Schwartz invited me into her ground floor apartment for a cup of tea. I accepted with relief, even though I knew she probably wanted to get me alone in order to describe some new problem I certainly couldn't solve. She moved slowly, using a walker. As she let herself into her triple-locked door, I noticed that she kissed her fingers and ran them over the mezuzah. We never did that in my family. We never heeded any of the Jewish customs that are so familiar on the Lower East Side. Yet now that ancient tribute to order and stability at home filled me with a searing, reflexive, almost racial grief for all those old people lost here in America.

In the shtetl, their age would have been taken as a mark of wisdom, or at least as an acceptable stage of human development, not as a burden that was too great for many of their offspring to bear. They would have lived with their children and their grandchildren, quarreling, of course, but accepting generational battles as a natural part of existence. They wouldn't have aged in terrified isolation, but remained part of a coherent community with familiar institutions, legends and ceremonies to comfort even those with the worst luck, the most debilitating physical and mental ailments. Beggars and rich men, cripples, fools and sages all shared the joy of the Sabbath, the sorrow of Yom Kippur, the crazy, rollicking abandon of Purim. On the Sabbath, some of the old men who'd begged for my attention in the project courtyard would have known the mellow pride of hearing their grandsons recite the week's lessons from Torah. Some of the women would have confidently supervised the complex preparations for the day of rest. And day after day their specific talents, like Moishe Kimmel's gift for crafting things, would have remained skills that were useful to the entire community, not just private isolated hobbies that seem a little sad and quirky when someone like Moishe boasts about them to an outsider. Those are the assumptions, the traditions, that the people who'd been clamoring for my attention still carried in their pores. But they'd gotten lost somewhere along the migrants' 50-year voyage into Modern America. The people I was meeting were part of a generation that was still in the desert.

Mrs. Schwartz offered me some tea and on old, crumbling piece of pound cake, in a voice that sounded more wheedling than courteous. It looked completely unappetizing to me, though I realized that buying it had probably meant a painful, scary journey across Henry Street to the nearest food store. She was probably saving it as an after-dinner treat. It all seemed so desperate, so hopeless, that I suddenly wanted to flee: the hell with my sociological sentimentality. Still, I accepted the cake since I feared she'd take a refusal of her food as a sign that I was refusing her as a person. And I listened to her story. She'd been chased out of the shtetl by a Russian pogrom in 1906. Her father, whose cousin had been involved in anti-government activities, had decided to flee before the Tsar's police arrested him. He found work in a Lower East Side grocery store, sleeping on Broome Street—literally on the street—so he could send enough money to bring his wife and kids over here. Those were hellish years in Russia for Mrs. Schwartz. She only survived because a gentile neighbor allowed her entire family to squeeze itself into the chimney of the small peasant house whenever the police drew near. Sometimes they'd hide there for three or four hours at a time. Mrs. Schwartz still has nightmares of those days.

She's lived on the Lower East Side ever since she moved to this country. She quit school at 14 in order to help her father, who'd opened his own small grocery store by then.

She married at 20, but her husband, a sickly man, never found a steady job, though he did get work at a small neighborhood newsstand whenever business was good. He died 15 years later. The couple never had any children. For the next 30 years Mrs. Schwartz worked as a ticket-taker in a Loew's theatre. She has lived in the Vladeck ever since it opened.

In June 1964, she had a stroke. Two nephews, both prosperous doctors, paid her medical bills. But they don't assist her or visit her any more. "What do they want with an old lady like me?" she asks. "Anyway, I have enough in the bank to pay for my rent and my food and buy my tombstone. What else do I need?" She has a few good friends left in the project. But most of them died or moved away years ago.

It is hard for her to sleep at night. She goes to bed at 7 or 8, but usually wakes up at midnight. Then, her aches, her fear that each fresh pain may bring a lonely death, keep her up for hours. She'd like to watch the Late Movie, but never turns the T.V. on for fear of angering her neighbors. She doesn't read much English, but she is able to spend a few agreeable hours reading the *Daily Forward*. It reminds her of the time when, as a teenager, she used to read the paper's most popular feature, "A Bintel Brief," a column of advice for immigrants, to her illiterate mother.

Now she gets the paper from an old Jewish war veteran she's known for years. He buys it on the street each morning and gives it to her each night before dinner. "He isn't all there either. I think he was shell-shocked." She says he drools when he talks and repeats himself constantly. She's very nervous anyway, and sometimes she feels as if his repetitions are making her so irritable she'll have another stroke. But she doesn't want to hurt the old man's feelings, or make him so angry he'll quit giving her his used *Forwards*.

She uses several kinds of medication each day—heart pills, painkillers, pills for high blood pressure. But on

April 1 her Medicaid ran out, though she had enough pills for another six months. That was what she wanted to tell me about. Whenever she goes to the local clinic to ask for a new application form to send in, they tell her she'll have to go to the main office on 34th Street. "But how can I get there? Do they think I can climb up and down the subway stairs? That I can afford to pay for a taxi? I telephone the office on 34th Street. But they always give me one of those recordings that say so-and-so is too busy to speak to me now. They must be very busy up there. I've called six times and I've always been cut off before I can talk to someone. I can't afford to waste all those dimes.

"Anyway, what good would it do me to reach them? The same thing always happens when I talk to people from the city. I get so flustered I begin to cry. Then I can't remember any English. The only words that come to me are in Yiddish. But everyone down there only speaks English or Spanish. What should I do? Some night I can't sleep at all. I'm so worried about what will happen to me if the pills I have now run out and I don't get a new supply."

The Hasidic Poor in New York City

Phyllis Franck

Their long black coats turning them into silhouettes, the bearded men hurry past decaying brownstone houses on their way to synagogue for evening services. In the morning, well before the work day starts, they will walk the same paths for the early services, and again in the evening, and then all day on Saturday, the Sabbath. It is an endless cycle learned from their fathers and passed down to their sons. This is the Hasidic section of New York in the Williamsburg section of Brooklyn, where 25,000 ultra-orthodox Jews live without televisions, movies or miniskirts, in what they feel is a special union with God.

They came to New York in the 1940s, to escape the Nazi persecutions in Europe, and have managed to carry on religious practices, traditions and a manner of dress much as their ancestors did when this sect first developed in Eastern Europe and Russia during the early eighteenth century. The Hasidim were glad to find a home where they were free from the fear of persecution, but they were not and still are not anxious to become Americanized, if that means giving up their traditions.

Unlike other recent immigrant groups who are now producing first and second generations in America, they complain of no identity crisis among their children, no generation gap between parent and child, and only vague fears that the children might get "ideas" and leave the orthodox way of life. Unlike other orthodox sects, out-migration of young people from the community is a minor problem. On the contrary, it is not unusual to hear the remark, "He is more Hasidic than his father." But because they are different, they have not been able to fully participate in the economic life of this country.

The more orthodox a Jew is in his practices, the more likely he is to be removed from the economic mainstream, and the Hasidic Jew is an extreme example. It would be unfair to plead poverty for the entire Hasidic community, as it would be unfair to say that they are the only Jews who are poor. But the fact is that many Hasidic Jews are poor. They have large families. Kosher foods are very expensive. The hours they work and their appearance prevent them from being hired in jobs where they are visible. In addition, for many who speak Yiddish and Hungarian, English is a second language. Thus men are forced to accept jobs as assembly line operators, where their appearance or command of the language is not important. Many of these jobs are now being replaced by machines.

Mrs. Shapiro and her husband and eight children live in one of those decaying old brownstones on Lee Avenue with all of the gargoyles and carvings. The peelings on the wrought iron trimmings reveal that they have been repainted innumerable times, but the owner has finally given up. The Shapiros live down a long, dark, musty corridor and past a creaky staircase in a first floor apartment, where they have lived since they were married 18 years ago.

Mrs. Shapiro, an attractive woman of about 38, wears a head scarf in the house, and a wig, called a *sheitel,* on the streets. (When a Hasidic woman marries, she must keep her hair covered at all times out of modesty.) Somewhat hesitantly, she explains that she was born to an Orthodox Jewish family in Germany. She was not Hasidic, but when she was 19 she was matched with a Hasidic man. They liked each other and were soon married. Since her marriage she has led a strict Hasidic life; she has not been to a movie, or danced with a man. Her husband worked for 12 years in a plastics company, doing a job that was recently taken over by a machine. The father of eight children, he is now learning a new job as an operator in a sweater factory. Her sister's husband, also Hasidic, has been living on the meager salary paid him by a synagogue to "sit and study." However, with a growing family, he too must look for a new job.

What insurance company wants to hire a man with side curls to sell its policies? What businessman is going to dismiss an employee at noon Fridays so that he can hurry home to prepare for his Sabbath, when he can't even make up the time on Saturday?

To a certain extent, Hasidic Jews have developed an economy within their own religious community. There are the kosher butcher shops, restaurants and bakeries, the silversmith who makes wine glasses and candlesticks, and the scribe who puts together religious books. Some Hasidic Jews make a living by selling items of a religious significance. One man operates a Kosher pizza shop, another invented the *Shabbos Zeiger*—the Sabbath Watcher—a device which turns the thermostat in the refrigerator on and off periodically so that when you open the refrigerator on Saturday, you are not starting a current, or "doing work". Others work as teachers in Hasidic schools.

The educational system of the Hasidic Jews places the main emphasis on religious study. It does not prepare them to participate in the economic world outside of their community. Their appearance does not allow them to do this, and their own small economy is not enough to absorb them. Their solution to poverty in the community is based on an old Biblical injunction. Ask any Williamsburg Jew about poverty and welfare and the standard answer is a rather defensive "We take care of our own." This is not always possible, but the idea has practical roots as well as religious ones. They have had to trust each other, in order to survive.

The Hasidim, which translated from Hebrew means "the Pious," came to America because of the Nazis. But they first came into existence as a reaction to an earlier reign of terror. In the late 1600s in Poland, prosperous and educated Jewish communities were raided by bands of Cossacks and Polish peasants who resented the fact many Jews held the privileged job of tax collector. Looking for deliverance, the shattered Jewish communities accepted the message of a man named Shabbtai Zvi, who claimed to be the Messiah. When he turned out to be a fraud, many Jews, disillusioned with a religion that had failed them, turned their backs on traditional Jewish scholarship. In its place they accepted a more mystical religion in which people could communicate directly with God and drive away evil spirits through songs and mystical formulas.

The founder of Hasidim was Israel of Moldavia, born in 1700 in Poland. He lived in a little hut in the forest so he could be close to nature. He spread the doctrine of love and taught that all Jews could reach God simply through prayers, without scholarship. He was called the Baal Shem Tov, the Master of the Good Name, because he could manipulate the letters of the mystical names of God as a type of divination.

Hasidim held so much greater appeal to the masses of Jewish laborers and artisans, the nonintellectuals, than the hair-splitting study and interpretation of the Torah (scriptures), the laws and the Biblical commentaries that by the end of the eighteenth century there was a deep schism in Eastern European Jewry. About one half of the Jews had become Hasidic. As Hasidim became less of a reaction and more a religion, there was a leveling off among its adherents between purely mystical prayer and the need for religious studies. Hasidic men today actually spend their lives studying, since Hasidim now means strict adherence to the letter of Jewish law as it is written.

When the Hasidim began to come to New York during and after World War II, they crossed the East River into Williamsburg. During the major Jewish migrations between 1899 and 1914, the new arrivals went to the Lower East Side. A people without a homeland, most Jews were anxious to learn English and assimilate. They condescendingly called the new Jewish immigrants who came after them "greenhorns."

The Jews were followed into the Lower East Side first by the Italians, and then the Puerto Ricans. With the arrival of these new groups and the completion of the bridge over the East River, the Jews began to move to the elegant but aging brownstone homes left by wealthy people who were moving out of Williamsburg. They built synagogues and Yeshivot (religious day schools). They opened kosher butcher shops and established societies to aid the sick and the needy. So the Hasidim came to Williamsburg, where it would be easiest to begin a new life within the old institutions. But even the Orthodox Jews of Williamsburg, who formed a buffer between the Hasidim and the rest of secular New York, had become too assimilated in the eyes of the Hasidim. Once they got their feet on the ground they opened their own schools, their own stores and their own bakeries and meat shops which were "glat kosher," more kosher than kosher.

Most Hasidim look askance at other Jews and feel that their way of being Jewish is the only way. Most of the rest of the six million Jews in America, whether Orthodox, Conservative, Reform or nonaffiliated, think that the Hasidim are dogmatic. The Hasidim won't use Hebrew as a conversational language, because it is the sacred tongue of the Bible. They often go beyond the biblical proscriptions in other ways, as well. But despite all of this, other Jews admire the strong devotion of the Hasidim to the family and their ability to maintain the strictest adherence to religious law in the face of every possible distraction that the modern world can offer. They have never tried to hide their religious identity as many American Jews have.

Little has been written about the Hasidic community in Williamsburg, because they do not want to be written about. Interviews are considered an intrusion on their privacy and a reporter trying to write an article about them learns to respect that feeling. One adequate study of the community was done by Solomon Poll, an assistant professor of sociology at the University of Pennsylvania. The study took him and several graduate students five years to complete. Although he has a thorough knowledge of Hebrew, Yiddish and Hungarian, and attended a Hasidic rabbinical school in Hungary, he devotes a whole chapter of his book to the problems of doing a study in Williamsburg. He said that even a Jewish writer has problems. If he is really religious he shouldn't have to ask such questions, and if he isn't religious then he is too far gone to bother with.

The work week for a Hasidic Jew ends around noon on Friday so that he can be home for the Sabbath before sundown. The men will go to synagogue for the evening service and come home to meals of chicken soup, roast meat, potato pudding, wine and egg bread, prepared on ovens lit before sundown, because lighting a cooking fire is a violation of the Sabbath. Candles are lit and a blessing said over the wine to usher in the Sabbath.

On Saturday, while the rest of New York is bustling with activity, happy to have a day when the stores are opened and the offices closed, Williamsburg is quiet. In the morning the men and children are in the synagogues praying. Many of the women remain home to prepare for the afternoon meal. In the late afternoon the men stroll the uneven flag-stone sidewalks or gather in small groups to chat. The men with the large, flat sable hats and long, silk top coats—the ones with the most severe expressions on their faces—are Rebbes, the spiritual leaders of the various congregations which have names like Satmar, Wishnitz and Pupa, the European or Russian communities from which the Hasidim have migrated.

There are many rabbis in the community—they are the slaughterers of kosher meat, the teachers, and the performers of circumcisions—but there are few Rebbes. The distinction is that the Rebbi—like the Baal Shem Tov—is given divine power by God. He has gained his position through heredity and his oldest son will continue the dynasty.

Groups of teenage girls stroll the streets and, except for a lack of makeup and their longer skirts, they look like most girls their age. But they never stop to chat with the men; women are considered a distraction to the man's world of study and prayer. Boys and girls are educated in separate schools. Men and women do not sit together in the synagogues. It is a community where marriages are made by matchmakers, and young women and men seldom meet more than once or twice before their wedding day. A classic remark by one Hasidic mother whose 19-year old son was still unmarried was, "I am worried about my David, that he isn't married. I can't seem to find him a wife. Either I don't like the mother or I don't like the father."

At sundown in all of the Jewish homes there will be a ceremony called the Havdala to usher out the Sabbath and usher in a new week; a work and school week which starts on Sunday morning. In the Hasidic schools the primary emphasis is on learning the Torah, the prayers and Jewish Law. Although New York state law requires them to have some nonreligious courses, the children know from the start that the subjects taught to them by the aging bearded rabbis are far more important to them than those taught by the outsiders.

Rabbi Bernard Weinberger, President of the Rabbinical Alliance of America, an Orthodox but not a Hasidic Rabbi who has a congregation in Williamsburg, has become the advocate of the poor Jews.

There is a refusal to recognize that the Jews are in the same box with other poor people. Orthodox life, especially Hasidic life, is such that you can't extricate yourself from religious values. Jews have had trouble becoming recipients of anti-poverty money, because the government claims that the problems are self-imposed, not treatable by the government. This is partially true, because there is a great pride that causes them to resist welfare.

A Jew will work 70 hours a week to eke out a living, because of his determination to sustain a family. He will work Saturday nights and Sunday, so long as he has his Sabbath. What the Hasidim need are training programs for good jobs that will accept them as they look. They already have an organized community.

Although everyone in the community, no matter how rich or poor, is called upon to contribute to community charities, Rabbi Weinberger emphasizes that these are only stop-gap measures and don't solve the basic problem of lack of jobs. In addition to the charities, there is also the strong family unit and the resourcefulness and industriousness of the Hasidic housewife to help relieve the sting of poverty.

Mrs. Shapiro exemplifies this. The Shapiros are on a waiting list for an apartment in a public housing project where they will have more rooms and more conveniences. Their present apartment, though small, is immaculately clean. The dining room buffet is like the family altar. It is covered with silver candle sticks, the kind that are used on Friday night to bench lecht—light the Sabbath candles. There are menorahs to hold the Hanukah lights. The large break front is where the dog-eared volumes of the books of the Torah, the Talmud and the prayer books which have been in the family for generations and endlessly pored over by the men of the family are kept. Mrs. Shapiro embroidered a beautiful tablecloth especially for the Sabbath, which she likes to show to guests. She is also proud of the clothing that she makes from fabrics bought for next to nothing at local bazaars. She makes almost all of her own clothes.

The Shapiros, of course, send all of their children to private religious schools, which are costly. Some of them are on scholarships. But Mrs. Shapiro saves additional money by making all of her own baked goods—six egg breads just for the Sabbath alone. She also buys things like potatoes and onions by the sack.

Her two oldest sons, 15 and 17, are on scholarships studying in a Hasidic Yeshiva in Israel. With a faraway look in her eyes, Mrs. Shapiro said, "I am very proud of them. One of them draws very well. He will probably be a sofer—a scribe." Then a little more quietly she said, "The older one can do anything. He knows all about the news, Nixon and the phantom jets for Israel, and he can build anything. He could be an architect." Then as if she shouldn't have said that, she added, "I have no say in these matters. He wants to study. Both my boys are religious."

Some families have left the community of Williamsburg, but few have given up their original way of life. Small settlements have sprung up in other parts of Brooklyn, but the people come to Williamsburg for groceries and send their children to school there. What is it that holds the Hasidim, with all of the distractions that surround them? Most likely it is the strong social control exerted by their religious mores, with rules and regulations that determine practically every action. There is a built-in security about such a life, in which few choices have to be made. It is a life that is so insulated, that it would be difficult to leave. There is also a special attraction about a mystical religion in which some people have divine authority. But some of the controls that have helped to maintain the community have also made it difficult for outsiders to help with programs that alleviate poverty.

There were no outside programs for poor Jews predating

the Office of Economic Opportunity, and there is still very little anti-poverty money in the Jewish community. This is partially because the community is so insulated that it was only when poor blacks and Puerto Ricans living in Williamsburg began to receive aid that the problems of the Hasidim came to light.

A social worker in the Jewish community is generally not trained in the practices of the community. He might arrange for commodity foods or food stamps for a Hasidic family, when they can't eat the food because it isn't kosher. If a woman social worker knocks on the door and a man is the only one home, he will probably slam the door in her face. She may think he is resisting therapy, when he is only abiding by the stricture not to talk to women. When OEO programs first became available, meetings and classes were often scheduled on nights on which Jews could not participate.

Since then programs have been adapted to the needs of of the community. Now there is an OEO-funded secretarial school, a family service program, a Head Start program and a small CAP program. An IBM computer training program was designed specifically with the Hasidim in mind. It was started in October with a $100,000 Department of Labor Manpower grant and the guidance of a private social science research organization called Urban Resources.

Computers are an ideal field for the Hasidim. Because of the mental gymnastics involved in Talmudic studies, they develop logical minds and score well on IBM aptitude tests. There is a dire need for programmers. Because the machines are kept running 24 hours a day, they must be constantly manned. This way a Hasidic Jew can adhere to his Sabbath and holidays and still work a 40-hour week. There is rapid mobility in the field, with starting salaries between $6,000 and $7,000 per year. During the 39-week training program, which meets Sunday through Thursday, the men receive a weekly training allowance of $45 for the first five weeks plus $5 for each dependent. After the first five weeks the basic rate goes up to $55. The men find time to continue their Talmudic studies in the morning and evenings and take breaks during the day for prayers.

The Hasidic Jew feels he is compromising his religion to an extent to participate in the program. But in most cases he has made the choice between sacrificing tradition or poverty. One man said, "If I don't talk to the women I work with, they will think I don't like them, and that has nothing to do with it. I am not supposed to talk to women, but I will if it is business."

As more job training programs become available for Hasidic Jews, other compromises may be required of them. Perhaps, like other groups before them, they will gradually exchange the old methods of survival for new ways. Whether in the face of this they will be able to maintain the social and religious control that has kept them intact for over two centuries is a question that only time will answer.

2. THE JEWISH RESPONSE TO THE JEWISH POOR

Some Aspects of the Jewish Attitude Toward the Welfare State

Isadore Twersky

The Jewish theory of philanthropy (*tzedakah; chesed*)—
or humanity, i.e., helping those who need help[1]—has
often been discussed and analyzed.[2] Its central position in
Jewish life and its concomitant importance in Jewish
literature[3] starting in the Biblical period and continuing
through talmudic times into the modern era, is copiously
documented.[4] Many rabbinic statements which stress,
with much verve and persuasiveness, the axial role of chesed
are frequently quoted[5]; for example, the dictum that
"charity is equivalent to all the other religious precepts
combined" (*Bava Batra* 9a) or that "he who is merciful
to others, mercy is shown to him by Heaven, while he
who is not merciful to others, mercy is not shown to him
by Heaven" (*Shabbat* 151b). I have no intention of reviewing all these examples. My aim is simply to describe the
metaphysical foundation of charity and to underscore a few
basic concepts, whose implications for Jewish social justice and welfare are as profound as they are pervasive,
by interpreting one striking talmudic passage, a dialogue
between the second-century sage R. Akiba and the Roman
general Turnus Rufus who was governor of the Judean
province. This historical fragment embodies the quintes-
sence of a Judaic social ethic: the special role of man in the
world, resulting from his practice of philanthropy; and
the relation of men to each other.

It has been taught: R. Meir used to say: "The critic [of Judaism] may bring against you the argument, 'If your God loves the poor, why does He not support them?' If so, answer him, 'So that through them we may be saved from the punishment of Gehinnom.' This question was actually put by Turnus Rufus to R. Akiba: 'If your God loves the poor, why does He not support them?' He replied, 'So that we may be saved through them from the punishment of Gehinnom.' 'On the contrary,' said the other, 'it is this which condemns you to Gehinnom. I will illustrate by a parable. Suppose an earthly king was angry with his servant and put him in prison and ordered that he should be given no food or drink, and a man went and gave him food and drink. If the king heard, would he not be angry with him? And you are called "servants," as it is written, *For unto me the children of Israel are servants.*' R. Akiba answered him: 'I will illustrate by another parable. Suppose an earthly king was angry with his son, and put him in prison and ordered that no food or drink should be given to him, and someone went and gave him food and drink. If the king heard of it, would he not send him a present? And we are called "sons," as it is written, *Sons are ye to the Lord your God.*' He said to him: 'You are called both sons and servants. When you carry out the desires of the Omnipresent, you are called "servants." At the present time you are not carrying out the desires of the Omnipresent.' R. Akiba replied: 'The Scripture says, *Is it not to deal thy bread to the hungry and bring the poor that are cast out to thy house.* When "dost thou bring *the poor who are cast out to thy house?* Now; and it says [at the same time],Is it not to deal thy bread to the hungry?"' [6]

The first premise to emerge from this dialogue is that *chesed* is that distinctive function which legitimatizes our worldly existence and adds a new dimension of purposiveness to life. It constitutes a special challenge and a unique prerogative[7] for man, by establishing him as a powerful agent and a delicate instrument in the conduct of human affairs. God has abdicated part of His function in order to enable man to continue and extend creation.[8] It is our practice of kindness which enables us to continue God's creative plan, elevates our life from brutishness to sensitivity, and extricates us from chaotic, vacuous biological existence. Indeed, man was created only on the assumption that he would passionately pursue chesed[9] and this, in turn, saves him from damnation and perdition.

This axial role of chesed is underscored in many other ways, among which the following is probably the most notable. While all religious-ethical actions are based on the principle of "imitation of God" (*imitatio dei* or *mimesis theou*), of walking in His ways and assimilating His characteristics,[10] this is especially true of chesed in its broadest sense. Chesed is the most emphatic of God's attributes (*rav chesed*); the world came into existence because of chesed; the majority of God's actions toward man are characterized by chesed.[11] The Torah begins and ends with loving-kindness as a divine act.[12] The practice of chesed thereby becomes man's "most God-like act."[13]

However, this is not the complete picture. Aiding the needy in all forms is not only a fulfillment of *imitatio dei*, but it is also comparable to aiding God Himself. The same R. Akiba whose dialogue with Rufus we are trying to interpret, dramatically deepens the social ethos of Judaism by equating charity to the poor with a loan to God.[14] We are accustomed, on the basis of halakhic terminology and conceptualization, to thinking of God as the ultimate "recipient" or "beneficiary" of all things "consecrated" for the Temple or other religious causes, all priestly gifts (tithe, heave-offering, etc.). God is the juridical personality that is the "owner," agent, or trustee of these things, and all legal procedures are based on this fact. Now, in R. Akiba's homily, God appears also as the ultimate "beneficiary" of gifts to the poor.[15] This involvement of God is certainly the noblest endorsement of that loving-kindness practiced between men.

Now let us return to the second feature of the dialogue.

At issue between the two disputants is the point of departure for determining human relationships. For R. Akiba, we are all brothers, because we are all children and, therefore, completely equal before God.[16] The brotherhood of man and fatherhood of God are inseparable. Any system which denies the common origin of man in God eviscerates the idea of brotherhood. Any system which affirms it must logically and inevitably sustain its corollary. The coordinates of the human system, in this view, are both horizontal and vertical and together create a relationship which results both in mutual responsibility and overlapping concern for each other. Even in a period of disgrace, disenchantment, or repudiation (such as exile or impoverishment), this relationship is not nullified and its demands not relaxed. Our identity as children and brothers is never obscured.[17] It is notable that the author of this statement, the great martyr who witnessed and experienced persecution and bestiality, was the one who articulated: "Beloved is man who was created in the image of God." His ethical objectivity was unaffected by oppression, his view of man and hierarchy of values was firm. Man to him was a unique figure.

For Rufus, on the other hand, only one aspect of the vertical relationship between man and God is determinative: that of submission and slavery. And did not Aristotle already proclaim that "slaves are like animals"? And had not Plato defined the slave as a "species of tame animal?"[18] If, then, the world—in this case, the Jewish community—is a large household inhabited by a mass of unrelated individuals, mere biological atoms, there can be no community of interests and responsibilities, no compassion and cooperation.

Implicit in R. Akiba's exchange with the Roman governor of Palestine is also a realistic-pragmatic view of the situation, a view which is sensitively attuned to suffering and privation and earnestly questing for improvement and fulfillment. The discussion here is not oriented to metaphysics; it is geared to ethics, to concrete social problems—something which is characteristic of talmudic discussion generally. It implies that one cannot conveniently fall back upon religious assumptions in order to justify passivity and resignation when confronted with social and ethical indignities. We must not look upon trouble impassively, whether the motivation be determinism (this is God's decree), condescension (some people are irretrievably singled out for subjection), or contemptuousness (physical-carnal matters are insignificant).[19] Poverty and inequality are pervasive—and will perhaps endure forever[20]—but they must be incessantly condemned and combatted. Judaism insists that man is obligated to mitigate injustice and alleviate suffering. There is, if you like, something antithetical in this situation. Poverty or sickness may be viewed as divine punishment or a form of retribution, just as wealth and health may be construed as signs of divine favor or reward.[21] Indeed, given a theocentric-teleological view of life, every episode or situation—including exile and death is divinely purposive.[22] Man, however, must not sit in judgment from such a theistic perspective; he should not approach poverty or sickness as predetermined criminal or punitive situations. A providential view of history is no excuse for quietism and no pretext for withdrawal.

Similarly, it seems to follow that one cannot dismiss a destitute person with a counterfeit expression of faith: "Rely on God, your father and king! He will help you." The cherished virtue of *bitachon*, trust, is something with which to comfort yourself in a time of depression, but it is not a pain-killing drug to be callously prescribed for others. If Reuben is starving, Simeon must provide food—not sanctimony. It is true that Reuben must live with hope and courage, but Simeon must act with dispatch and compassion. God's inscrutable benevolence is not a substitute for man's tangible benevolence. As R. Bachya ibn Pakuda observes,[23] bitachon has a multiplicity of implications: to the impoverished person it conveys the need for tranquillity, patience, and contentment with one's portion, while to the man of means, it suggests the obligation of sustained and gracious liberality.

Our cursory analysis of these concepts enables us, in conclusion, to pinpoint the unique feature of chesed, in contradistinction to other philanthropic systems. It would be gratuitous—and chauvinistic—to give Judaism an exclusive monopoly over the practice of charity; the rabbis, as a matter of fact, never denied that other nations were charitable.[24] Judaism's contribution is a new *motive* for philanthropy: the religious-humane motive, which means acting for the sake of humanity because of religious conviction and obligation. Humanity is an expression of piety ("Everyman who is endowed with loving kindness is without doubt a God-fearing man," *Sukkah* 49b); the two are absolutely inseparable. Commitment to God is inconceivable in Judaism without compassion for man. "Whoever turns his eyes away from [one who appeals for] charity is considered as if he were serving idols."[25] Philo describes philanthropy as "the virtue closest akin to piety, its sister and its twin," for "the nature which is pious is also humane, and the same person will exhibit both qualities of holiness to God and justice to man."[26] One cannot claim to be God-intoxicated without having an unquenchable thirst for social justice. Indeed, theological postulates sundered from their practical consequences are powerless, and perhaps—purposeless. They are mutually supplementary and independently fragmentary.[27]

This motive should be the propelling force of federation activities and should determine its welfare program.

Halakhah is a tense, vibrant, dialectical system, identifiable by its beautiful blend of romanticism and classicism. This is both cause and consequence of the halakhic insistence upon normativeness in action and inwardness in feeling and thought. The historic achievement of Halakhah was to move beyond theoretical principles of faith to a minutely regulated code of religio-ethical behavior—to give concrete and continuous expression to theological ideals, ethical norms and historical concepts. It is based upon the conviction that abstract belief, even an intensely personal or charismatic one, will be evanescent and that religious insight which is not firmly anchored down by practice is unreal. Its goal is spirituality together with conformity—"the saturation and transfusion of everyday life with the thought of God" (the felicitous phrase of a 19th century theologian, Bousset). This insistence upon the "coincidence of opposites" (call it law and prophecy, if you like, or institution and charisma, everyday life and the thought of God) creates the "dialectical pull" or tension which is characteristic of so many root principles and fundamental beliefs of Judaism.

A favorite example of this creative tension is the institution of prayer, which attempts to balance inward experience with routinized performance, to avoid an anarchic liturgy and at the same time not to produce a spiritless stereotype. In other words, the Halakhah takes a thesis—spontaneity of prayer, manifest in a genuinely dialogic relationship between man and God—superimposes upon it an antithesis—standardization and uniformity of prayer— and strives to maintain a synthesis: a devotional routine.

I would like to suggest that the institution of *tzedakah*—charity—provides an equally attractive illustration of this dialectical structure. The Halakhah undertook to convert an initially amorphous, possibly even capricious act into a rigidly defined and totally regulated performance. It made charitable contributions, usually voluntary in nature, obligatory, subject to compulsory assessment and collection. However, while objectifying and concretizing a subjective, fluid state of mind, it visited relentlessly upon the proper attitude, feeling, and manner of action. It hoped to combine the thesis of free, spontaneous giving with the antithesis of soulless, obligatory contribution and produce a composite act which is subjective though quantified, inspired though regular, intimate yet formal. As is the case with prayer and other products of such dialectical synthesis, the tension is very great, for the breakdown of the synthesis is always an imminent and immanent possibility. The pattern of behavior may become atrophied and de-spiritualized, or else the standardized practice may be overthrown. Here the tension is even reflected semantically in the term *tzedakah*, which means both righteousness and charity, an act based on one's moral conscience as well as an appropriate course of action spelled out in detail by the law. [28]

Within the practical-halakhic framework of philanthropy, this polarity comes to the surface in two main areas. First of all, there is the constant interplay between the individual and the community with regard to the responsibility for and awareness of philanthropic needs. A study of the laws of charity yields paradoxical conclusions. On the one hand, it seems that the central figure is the individual: to him the commandments are addressed, he is enjoined to engage unstintingly in charity work, and to assiduously help his fellow man. He is the hero of philanthropy, seeking exposure to needy people and responding effusively to their requests. On the other hand, it is surprising to find that the Halakhah has assigned an indispensable, all-inclusive role to the community. The community acts not only as a supervisory, enforcing agency but it also occupies the center of the stage as an entity possessed of initiative and charged with responsibility. One may persuasively argue that the Halakhah makes of philanthropy a collective project; philanthropic endeavor, long-term aid (*kupah*) as well as immediate, emergency relief (*tam-*

chuy), is thoroughly institutionalized. Responsibility for the care of the needy—sick, poor, aged, disturbed—is communal. The individual makes his contribution to the community chest and with this he apparently discharges his obligations. He acts mechanically, almost anonymously, by responding to the peremptory demands of the collectors "who go about among the people every Friday soliciting from each whatever is assessed upon him." Tzedakah thus emerges as an individual obligation which is fulfilled corporately. And it should be noted that this is a premeditated arrangement. The community does not step in and assume responsibility ex post facto, after individuals have shirked their duty or failed to manage matters properly. The community initially appears as a modified welfare city-state, with its special functionaries who collect the compulsory levy and act as trustees for the poor and needy.

This is the first expression of polarity between the individual and community.

Whoever continues to acquaint himself with *Hilkhot Tzedakah* in the *Shulchan Arukh* or *Matenot Aniyim* in the *Mishneh Torah* comes across another basic antithesis inherent in the very concept of charity. On the one hand, the Halakhah is interested only in the objective act, the amount given, meeting the challenge, and relieving the needs of the destitute. This is a complete, self-contained, determined act. On the other hand, we are confronted by an exquisitely sensitive Halakhah, very much concerned not only with *what* but also with *how* the act of charity is implemented. Not only the outward act is important; the experiential component is also significant. One need not rely upon the preacher's eloquence or the moralist's fervor to underscore the importance of motivation and attitude in the halakhic act of charity.

This correlation of the objective and subjective components within the individual act is the second area of tension and polarity between the individual and the community.

Let us take up these two points briefly and concretize them somewhat. We may illustrate the polarity of the community-individual partnership by introducing a few specific laws.

For example, the Mishnah states that 12 months residence is required before a man is counted as one of the townsmen and is obliged to support communal projects. The Talmud, however, goes on to cite another passage which differentiates between various levies. "A man must reside in a town thirty days to become liable for contributing to the soup kitchen, three months for the charity box,. . . and twelve months for contributing to the repair of the town walls."[29] The reason for the distinction between charity and communal enterprises is clear. Only after a man has become a full-fledged resident and has submitted to communal jurisdiction does he become liable to abide by communal ordinances (*takkanot bene ha-'ir*) and share communal expenses. Charity, though, is an individual obligation and one need not come under communal jurisdiction to be liable. At the same time, the community serves as the executive branch which organizes, implements and distributes charitable contributions.

The sense of communal involvement is projected even more in the following laws. "If the inhabitants of a city impose a charitable levy upon a visiting merchant, the contribution belongs to the poor of the city visited. If, however, the levy be imposed upon a visiting group of people, the contributing is done in the city visited, but the sum collected is conveyed, by the returning visitors, to the city of their origin that the poor of the latter city may be aided with that money."[30] Again, the reason for the differentiation between a wayfaring individual and an intinerant company is apparent. The individual relates to his immediate communal framework, and his charitable contribution is absorbed and disbursed there. A group of people are considered to have affiliations with both communities. They contribute immediately to demonstrate their solidarity with the new group and remove suspicion that they are tax dodgers, but return the money for distribution to their original community. What is significant is the permeative involvement with the community on all levels– the strong, ineradicable sense of community action.

So far the enterprising community is in the center, and the timid individual is on the periphery. It almost seems as though a man's obligation is terminated when he weighs the gold pieces or signs a check—and then, losing his identity, simply fades away into the shadows of the community. Now let us see how the relationship shifts gears, and hear the Halakhah insist that there are aspects of the commandment concerning charity which transcend the basic levy exacted by the community. The institution of *kupah* relieves only one's minimal, quantified duties, but other individual, contingent obligations are not superseded.

For example, the obligation of charity is based on both positive and negative commandments: "open thy hand unto him"; "thou shalt not harden thy heart nor shut thy hand" (cf. Leviticus 25:35; Deuteronomy 15:7-8). The nature of the relationship between such mutually reinforcing formulations—a *mitzvat 'aseh* and a *mitzvat lo ta'-aseh*—presents an halakhic problem. Some interpretations submit that the two are completely commensurate and the negative one has no intrinsic significance; it relates only to the omission of the positive—the failure to contribute. According to many talmudic authorities, however, the negative commandment not to harden one's heart relates exclusively to one's mental-emotional attitude when confronted with distress. It is addressed only to the individual, and stipulates that the individual should not be insensitive and nonresponsive to the plea of an indigent person—"a poor person in search of help." The positive commandment is in no way contingent upon the plea or request of the poor, while the negative commandment relates not only to the omission of the positive but is also an act of commission: of callously refusing the poor, of consciously hardening one's heart and thwarting one's inclination to kindness.[31]

What is more, if one has already given charity, even oversubscribed his quota, there is an additional law which states: "It is forbidden to turn away a suppliant poor person empty handed, though one grant no more than a single berry." This is based on Psalm 74:21: "Let not the oppressed turn back in confusion."[32]

The emphasis upon individual responsibility is thus unequivocal. However, we might go further and submit that according to the social ethos of Judaism, the individual can never really isolate himself from the needy, especially in times of euphoria, pleasure and indulgence. The very nature of rejoicing and festivity includes sharing with others. This axiom of kindness was formulated by Maimonides as follows. "While one eats and drinks by himself, it is his duty to feed the stranger, the orphan, the widow, and other poor and unfortunate people, for he who locks the doors to his courtyard and eats and drinks with his wife and family, without giving anything to eat and drink to the poor and the bitter in soul—his meal is not a rejoicing in a divine commandment, but a rejoicing in his own stomach . . . Rejoicing of this kind is a disgrace to those who indulge in it."[33]

It is noteworthy that in many cities—one of the earliest records is from Hamburg—a communal ordinance required every townsman to have two guests for the Sabbath.[34] Personal contact with and exposure to the needy was essential. "There was a certain pious man with whom Elijah used to converse until he made a porter's lodge [gatehouse] after which he did not converse with him any more" (because the poor men were shut out from the courtyard).[35] Sharing the companionship of the poor and making them socially equal is a highly sensitive performance which merits special blessing. "He who lets poor people and orphans partake of food and drink at his table shall call upon the Lord and find, to his delight, that the Lord will answer" (Is. 58:9).[36]

So, although the balance may be delicate and tense, corporate responsibility does not eclipse individual awareness and should not dull individual sensitiveness. This would remain true even if communal funds were somehow to become inexhaustible; individual obligations never cease.[37]

Let us return to the second expression of polarity—the objective act vis-à-vis the inner experience and accompanying attitude. As a general principle, we may study the assertion that "the reward of charity depends entirely upon the extent of the kindness in it."[38] The cold, formal, objective act does not suffice; it must be fused with warmth and loving-kindness. From an objective point of view, the giving of charity is not subject to qualifications; if you give, that's that, and the amount is the only thing that counts. From a subjective point of view, the same act may well be shoddy and meretricious. There can be such a thing as "defective charity." The difference is, if you like, whether there is a heart of flesh or a heart of stone behind it. Allow me to suggest perhaps that the difference expresses itself in the two expressions we have for this act: "giving charity" and "doing charity." "Doing" relates to the method and quality of "giving." "Giving" is concrete and limited; you give ten dollars or 100 dollars. "Doing" is how you go about it.

A late source gives this apt illustration.[39] "The giving is *tzedakah*. The doing is the trouble to bring it to the poor man's house, or the thoughtfulness on the part of the giver that it should be most useful . . . in short, being *preoccupied* with the good of the poor recipient." The key terms here are *tirchah* and *tirdah* which denote constant concern and abiding interest—continous commitment, rather than fleeting attention. The same idea of mental and emotional preoccupation is underscored by the recurrent idiom *osek be-Torah u'vigemilut chasadim*(preoccupation with Torah and acts of loving-kindness). *Osek* suggests a resilient, incompressible quality of attention and dedication; it negates the idea of a perfunctory, quantified act.[40]

There are a number of specific subjective features which may be collated under this general principle—that "the reward of charity depends entirely upon the extent of the kindness in it." Many of these features are embodied in Maimonides's original, well-known classification of the "eight degrees of benevolence, one above the other." Instead of reproducing this classification here it might be more useful to abstract from it and related source material a few characteristics and tendencies, which identify the experiential component of charity.

Most important is to approach the needy prudently, tactfully and graciously. "Happy is he that considereth the poor" (Psalm 41:2). The ultimate aim of this approach is to get the poor one to take a loan or else think that he is taking a loan, to accept him into business partnership or help him find employment. This completely eliminates or deftly camouflages humiliation and degradation. It rehabilitates, rather than aids, and avoids the most objectionable influences of pauperism.[41] In other words, it is not only ethically correct but is also economically sound. Is this not the ideal of all philanthropic federations?

If the humiliation attendant on receiving charity cannot be eliminated, it should be reduced as much as possible. This expresses itself above all in the secrecy and privacy of giving. "He who gives alms in secret is greater than Moses" (*Bava Batra* 9a).[42]

Another basic principle, which may be most relevant to

our experiences, is the insistence upon individual consideration of the needy, rather than indiscriminate handling of
them as so many "faces in the crowd." The indigent
remains a dignified individual, with his own needs and
drives, his own sensibilities and rights, strengths and weak-
nesses. The essence of the religious commandment is "to
assist a poor person according to his needs"—in other
words, selectively not uniformly. Regimentation or massive
institutionalization are not in keeping with this spirit.
You might find here an inferential endorsement of the
case-method of social work, being careful not to deper-
sonalize the individual client or blur his identity by mechanically bracketing him. If you like, we have here the social-
philanthropic repercussions of the metaphysical idea of
the dignity, worth, and uniqueness of each individual.

Also imperative is prompt, courteous attention, with
little or no "red tape," bureaucratic inefficiency or personal
procrastination. Delay in responding to a request may
blemish the entire act or even tragically obviate its need.
You know the "confession" of the sorely afflicted Nachum
ish Gamzu, who was "blind in both his eyes, his two hands
and legs were amputated, and his whole body was covered
with boils." He had wished this state upon himself after,
in his own words, "a poor man stopped me on the road
and said, 'Master, give me something to eat.' I replied:
Wait until I have unloaded something from the ass. I had
hardly managed to unload something when the man
died."[43]

The benevolent act should be gracious from beginning
to end and should not display half-heartedness or im-
patience. It is in this light that we understand one of the
commandments subsumed under the precept "Love thy
neighbor as thyself," namely the obligation to "escort the
strangers and departing guests." "Hospitality to wayfarers
is greater than receiving the Divine Presence . . . but escorting guests is even greater than according them hospitality

. . . Whoever does not accompany guests is as though he would shed blood.''[44] It would appear that hospitality without escorting is like throwing a bone to a dog—a begrudging concession of kindness, an intrinsically benevolent act which is vitiated by its rudeness.

Most striking because it is most intangible and "supra-legal," is the stipulation that actual giving be accompanied by sympathy, sharing the recipient's troubles, talking with him, relieving him psychologically. This calls for a genuine sense of commiseration. "He who gives a small coin to a poor man obtains six blessings, and he who addresses to him words of comfort obtains eleven blessings."[45] Maimonides sharpens this sentiment even more: "Though one were to give a thousand pieces of gold, one forfeits, yea, one destroys the merit of one's giving if one gives grudgingly and with countenance cast down." On the contrary, "one should give cheerfully and eagerly. One should grieve with the poor person over his misfortune [Job 30:25] and should address to him words of solace and of comfort" [Job 29:13][46]

The receiver must feel that there is a living human voice behind the grant, not a hollow, impersonal one. The donor should never lose sight of the fact that tzedakah is as much a "duty of the heart" as it is a "duty of the limb." Without these subjective elements, the objective act is deficient and sometimes even worthless.

Even though we have expanded its scope and insisted upon the place of subjectivity in it, we have been examining tzedakah almost exclusively. However, we should not fail to note that there is within the scope of chesed an entire area of acts of kindness where the personal subjective attitude is not only relevant but is of exclusive significance. This may be designated as "mental hygiene" (as distinct from physical aid and rehabilitation). Of the several categories of kindness referred to in the Talmud, two belong to this area: visiting the sick, and comforting the bereaved. These acts could also conceivably be regulated—

e.g., stipulating by communal ordinance that the sick should be visited right after the Sabbath morning service[47] —but clearly the physical act of entering the sick room, unlike the physical act of signing a check, is certainly not worthless. For these are "the deeds of loving-kindness performed in person and for which no fixed measure is prescribed." (*Hilkhot Avel* 14:1). The subjective moment is paramount.

Old-age care and consideration is another area in the realm of kindness and social welfare where the attitude outweighs or at least conditions the act.

This is true with regard to parents as well as aged people generally. We are obliged "to rise up before the gray-haired and honor the face of the old man." (Leviticus 20:32) There is nothing material in this. Financial assistance to poor old people is to be viewed from the general vantage point of charity. The specific obligation is the reverential attitude: to stand, to make respectful gestures. With regard to one's parents, the material assistance, when required, is probably also to be viewed from the vantage point of charity.[48] Indeed, the Halakhah states that honoring one's parents means providing them with food and drink, clothing and covering, but the expense is to borne by the parents. What counts, on the part of the son, is the zeal and quality of service. In other words, the fulfillment of "honoring thy father and mother" and "ye shall fear, every man, his mother and father" is not contingent upon finance. Indeed, since it was emphatically maintained that the honoring of parents was on a level with the honoring of God,[49] this could not be, in essence, a materially conditioned act. In socially ideal situations, where the parents have independent resources, the duty of honor and reverence is unimpaired and their scope unrestricted. The religious-social obligations toward an old person are the same regardless of whether he is independently wealthy, sustained by social security and old-age assistance, or indigent.

In this sense, welfare activities which tend to mitigate financial difficulties cannot be looked upon as corrosive of traditional values and obligations, because they do not impinge upon the core of philanthropic actions: the motif of personal service and attitude. Welfare activities are no more "dangerous" in theory than the activities of high-powered, mechanized philanthropy: both challenge the subjective element, both tend to neutralize or obliterate it. The response to this challenge will have to reaffirm that if Halakhah, generally, was intended to be an ongoing education in holiness and spiritual dedication, then tzedakah in particular was intended to be an education in kindness and all-consuming *humanitas*.

NOTES

[1]These two terms are used interchangeably by Philo; see Harry A. Wolfson, *Philo: Foundations of Religious Philosophy in Judaism, Christianity and Islam*, (Cambridge, Mass.: Harvard University Press, 1947), 2, p. 219.

[2]The following references are representative of the treatment of our theme in modern scholarly literature; they are not intended to provide a complete bibliography. I. Abrahams, *Jewish Life in the Middle Ages* (New York: Meridian Press, 1958), chs. 17–18; S. Baron, *The Jewish Community* (Philadelphia: Jewish Publication Society, 1942), vol. 2, ch: 16; J. Bergman, *Ha-Zedakah be-Yisrael* (Jerusalem, 1944; Hebrew); Israel Chipkin, "Judaism and Social Welfare," *The Jews*, ed. L. Finkelstein, (3rd ed. Philadelphia, Jewish Publication Society, 1960), vol. 2, pp. 1043–1075; A. Cronbach, *Religion and its Social Setting* (Cincinnati, Hebrew Union College, 1933), pp. 99–157; Ephraim Frisch, *An Historical Survey of Jewish Philanthropy* (New York, MacMillan, 1924); K. Kohler, "The Historical Development of Jewish Charity," *Hebrew Union College and other Addresses* (Cincinnati, Hebrew Union College, 1916), pp. 229–253; S. Schechter, "Notes of Lectures on Jewish Philanthropy," *Studies in Judaism*, 3rd series (Philadelphia: Jewish Publication Society, 1934), pp. 238–277.

[3]The following sources are most relevant: Mishnah, *Pe'ah*, 8:3–8 and Tosefta, *Pe'ah*, 4:9–11; Tosefta, *Megillah*, 3:4; *Bava Batra*, 8a–11a; *Ketuvot*, 67b–68a; *Kiddushin*, 30b–33a; *Bava Kamma* 36b (and

especially *Sefer ha-Ma'or and Milchamot, ad. loc.*); *Shir ha-Shirim Zuta*, ed. S. Buber (Vilna, Romm, 1925), pp. 17ff. Among the post-Talmudic codes: *Sefer ha-Eshkol*, ed. Shalom Albeck, I., (Jerusalem, Mass.), pp. 164 ff; *Mishneh Torah, Hilkhot Matenot Aniyim*, chs. 7–10; *Hilkhot Mamrim*, ch. 6; *Hilkhot Melakim*, ch. 10; *Or Zaru'a*, 1, *Hilkhot Tzedakah*, pp. 13–18; *Yoreh De'ah*, 247 ff. For more popular discussions or compendia of sayings, see *Sefer Hasidim* (Frankfurt, Wahrmann, 1924), n. 857 ff. (pp. 215 ff.); n. 1713 ff. (pp. 404 ff.); *Ma'alat ha-Midot* of R. Yehiel b. Yekutiel ha-Rofe, chs. 5 and 6; *Menorat ha-Ma'or* of R. Isaac Abuhab, *Ner 3, Kelal 8*; *Menorat ha-Ma'or* of R. Israel ibn al-Nakawa, ed. G. Enelow (New York, 1929), 1, pp. 23–90; *Netibot Olam* (Maharal of Prague), *Netib Gemilut Chesed*; R. Isaac Lampronti, *Pahad Yitzhak*, s.v. *tzedakah*. Of special interest is the *Me'il Tzedakah*, by R. Elijah ha-Kohen of Izmir.

Many of the talmudic sources have been discussed by Prof. E. E. Urbach in a very valuable article in *Zion*, 16 (1951), pp. 1–27. Mention should also be made of Prof. A. Cronbach's series of articles which appeared in the *HUCA* since 1925.

[4]The latest is Harry Lurie, *A Heritage Affirmed* (Philadelphia: Jewish Publication Society, 1961).

[5]Nachmanides observed: "Tzedakah is an equally severe [precept]; and with it there are many warnings and great stirring pronouncements in the Torah, the Prophets; the Sacred Writings and in the teachings of our Rabbis. With respect to the teachings of our Rabbis, I do not have to remind one of all of the sources that discussed the subject of Tzedakah because the entire Talmud and all the volumes of the *Aggados* are replete with this." (This, and subsequent Talmudic and Halachic quotations were translated from Hebrew and Aramic by Rabbi Samuel I. Cohen.) See *Derashat ha-Ramban le-Kohelet*, ed. Z. Schwarz (Frankfurt, Saenger, 1913), pp. 26, 28.

[6]Bava Batra 10a.

[7]See *Midrash Rabbah, Va-Yikra*, 34:8 (ed. M. Margaliyot, p. 791); *Tanhuma, Mishpatim*, 9; *Shir ha-Shirim Zuta*, p. 18.

[8]See the other dialogue between R. Akiba and Rufus. *Tanchuma Tazri'a*, 9 (ed. Buber, p. 18a).

[9]*Bereshit Rabbah*, 8:5.

[10]*Sotah* 14a; *Shabbat* 133b.

[11]See Maimonides, *Guide for the Perplexed*, 3, 53 and *Mishneh Torah, Hilkhot Megillah*, 2:17. Also Nachmanides, p. 26.

[12]*Sotah* 14a.

[13]The phrase is that of S. R. Hirsch, *Horeb*, vol. 2.

[14] *Bava Batra* 10a (in the name of R. Johanan); *Shir ha-Shirim Zuta*, p. 15.

[15] This homiletical motif can even be substantiated by halakhic norms. According to many Talmudic authorities, obligating oneself for charitable contributions conforms to the same procedure as consecrating objects to God. See Maimonides, *Hilkhot Mekhirah*, 22:15–16; Nachmanides, Commentary on Numbers, 30:3 (second explanation); and *Sefer ha-Ma'or* and *Milchamot* to *Bava Kamma* 36a. When speaking of "things which are for the sake of God," Maimonides mentions, all in the same breath, consecrating objects, constructing synagogues, and feeding the hungry; *Issurei Mizbeach*, 7:11.

[16] See also *Avot*, 3:18.

[17] This is the thrust of the end of the passage, emphasizing help to the poor when "they are cast out." It is also the theme of the talmudic discourse, "Feed me (at least) like a dog and like a raven" (*Bava Batra* 8). See also the view of R. Akiba in the Mishnah, *Bava Kamma* 8:6 ("Even the poorest in Israel are looked upon as freemen who have lost their possessions"). It is noteworthy that the Bible invariably uses the word "brother" when speaking of *tzedakah*.

Incidentally, Rufus's rejoinder probably mirrors the Christian polemic that exile is punishment, symbolizing the complete rejection of Israel.

[18] Aristotle, *Politics*, 1254; Plato, *Politics*, 289b, d. See, e.g. Glenn Morrow, *Plato's Law of Slavery in its Relation to Greek Law* (Urbana, University of Illinois, 1939).

[19] Judaism, for the most part, realistically negated asceticism, monasticism or any other contemptuous rejection of worldly matters (See. E. Urbach, "Ascesis and Suffering in Talmudic and Midrashic Sources" *Baer Jubilee Volume* [Jerusalem, 1960], 48–68). There is in Judaism no exaltation or idealization of poverty, such as we find in many Christian Systems of thought (see Troeltsch, *Social Teachings of the Christian Churches*, vol. 1). Poverty is not adored as a blessed state; it is an ugly, demeaning situation. One is duty-bound—so far as is humanly possible—to avoid falling into such a state; he who brings it upon himself by dissipating his resources is a fool (Maimonides, *Arakhin wa-Charamin*, 8:13). Diminution of wealth is not per se an act of piety or self-transcending religiosity (see *Kuzari*, 2, 50). "Holy voluntary poverty" (a basic concept of canon law) was neither an attraction or a goal for the Halakhah. It should be stressed, of course, that this emphatic point has its counterpoint: there is in Judaism no glorification of wealth as an end in itself. As a matter of fact, the unbridled pursuit of money is most objectionable. Wealth is a trust over which man is the executor; it

should be used imaginatively and wisely to uproot poverty. (*See Guide for the Perplexed*, 3, 35, and 39; *Yoreh De'ah*, 247:3. The "stewardship theory" of wealth as well as the cyclical view of human resources are commonplace.)

[20] *Shabat* 151b.

[21] See *Sukkah* 29a.

[22] *Chullin* 7b: "A man's finger will not be hurt in this world unless it was so ordained above."

[23] *Chovot Ha-Le-vavot, Sha'ar ha-Bitachon* (Warsaw, 1875, p. 202 f.). It is noteworthy that the Karaites promulgated an inflexibly passive, quietistic interpretation of *bitachon*; see now M. Zucker, (*On the Commentary of Rabbi Saudiah Gaon on the Torah*) pp. 205–207.

[24] The famous symposium between R. Johanan b. Zakkai and his disciples—*Bava Batra* 10a—focuses on this. See also S. Lieberman, *JQR*, 36 (1945–46), pp. 357–359; E. Urbach, *Zion*, p. 4, n. 23.

[25] *Bava Batra* 10a; *Koheleth Rabbah*, 7:1.

[26] See Wolfson, *Philo*, II, p. 219.

[27] See especially *Kiddushin* 31a, passage starting "Ulah learned, that which is written, 'All the kings of the earth shall praise thee, O Lord, when they hear the words of thy mouth.'"

[28] Perhaps it is this built-in tension which explains the view of those *rishonim* (see *Tosafot, Ketuvot* 49b) who maintain that although charity is obligatory, it is not enforceable in court, but can be collected only with the help of moral suasion and social sanction. This preserves a "subjective" element. Even more striking is an apparent incongruity in the view of Maimonides. In common with most halakhists he assumes that charity is subject to compulsory assessment and collection. (See *Matenot Aniyim*, 7:10 and *Ketzot ha-Choshen, Yoreh De'ah*, 290). Yet, in the *Moreh Nebukhim* (3, 53) he differentiates between *tzedek* and *tzedakah*; *tzedek* is legally prescribed and regulated while *tzedakah* stems from one's moral conscience. There is an ethical increment, something more than and different from the formalized, purely legal act.

[29] *Bava Batra* 7b, 8a.

[30] *Matenot Aniyim*, 7:14; see *Or Zaru'a*, I, p. 15.

[31] See *Tosafot, Bava Batra* 8b (the views of R. Tam and Ri); *Matenot Aniyim*, 7:2; *Sefer Yere'im, amud* 5, n. 202 (p. 182).

[32] *Matenot Aniyim*, 7:7.

[33] *Yom Tov* 6:18; see also *Megillah* 2:17.

[34] See *Yoreh De'ah*, 256:1 and commentaries; *Menorat ha-Ma'or, Ner* 3, *Kelal* 7; Bergmann, *Ha-Tzedakah be-Yisrael*, p. 143.

[35] *Bava Batra* 7b.

[36] *Matenot Aniyim*, 10:16.

[37] It is important for welfare workers to remember that distribution of funds is a more exacting task than collection—no matter how important the latter may be substantively and sociologically (as a cohesive force). Allocation of funds, requiring serious deliberation and penetrating evaluation, is halakhically and ethically the most responsible task; allocation committees are in the most delicate, or vulnerable, position. See the Halakhot concerning: "A money box for Tzedakah should be collected by two people and distributed by three people."

[38] *Sukkah* 49b.

[39] *Pachad Yitzhak*, s.v. *tzedakah*.

[40] The beautiful passage (*Abot de R. Natan,* 7) which contrasts the benevolence of Abraham with that of Job points up, in its own homiletical idiom and cadence, the qualitative difference between bland "giving" and inspired "doing."

> Now when that great calamity came upon Job, he said unto the Holy One, blessed be He: "Master of the Universe, did I not feed the hungry and give the thirsty to drink; as it is said, *Or have I eaten my morsel myself alone and the fatherless hath not eaten thereof* (Job 31:17)? And did I not clothe the naked, as it is said, *And if he were not warmed with the fleece of my sheep*" (Job 31:20)?
> Nevertheless the Holy One, blessed be He, said to Job: "Job, thou hast not yet reached half the measure of Abraham. Thou sittest and tarriest within thy house and the wayfarers come in to thee. To him who is accustomed to eat wheat bread, thou givest wheat bread to eat: to him who is accustomed to eat meat, thou givest meat to eat; to him who is accustomed to drink wine, thou givest wine to drink. But Abraham did not act in this way. Instead he would go forth and make the rounds everywhere, and when he found wayfarers he brought them into his house. To him who was unaccustomed to drink wine, he gave wine to drink. Moreover he arose and built stately mansions on the highways and left there food and drink, and every passerby ate and drank and blessed Heaven. That is why delight of spirit was vouchsafed to him. And whatever one might ask for was to be found in Abraham's house, as it is said, *And Abraham planted a tamarisk tree in Beer-Sheba*" (Gen. 21:33). Tr. by J. Goldin, (Yale University Press, 1959), p. 47.

See also *Sotah* 10b; *Shabbat* 104a.

[41] This was noticed by perceptive observers. For example, Beatrice Webb concludes her description of the Jewish Board of Guardians in England as follows: "While all groundwork for the charges of pauperi-

zation is absent, we have conclusive evidence that either from the character of those who take, or from the method of those who give, Jewish charity does not tend to the demoralization of individual recipients."

[42]Very beautiful is the midrashic explanation, adopted by Rashi and other commentators, of the last verse in Ecclesiastes. Whereas the standard translation reads: "For God shall bring every work into the judgment concerning every hidden thing, whether it be good or whether it be evil," the midrashic translation would read: "concerning every hidden thing which is *both* good and evil." And what constitutes a "thing which is both good and evil"—giving charity publicly! See also *Chagigah* 5a.

[43]*Taanit* 21a.

[44]Maimonides, *Hilkhot Avel*, 14:2. See also Rashi, *Sotah* 10a, explanation of Eh-shel.

[45]*Bava Batra* 9b.

[46]*Matenot Aniyim*, 10:4. See *Sefer Mitzvot Gadol.* n. 289 "And thy heart shall not be grieved when thou givest unto him." *Guide for the Perplexed*, 2, 39.

[47]See *Or Zaru'a*, 2, 51.

[48]This is a moot point halakhically. We may discern three basic views: see *Tosafot, Kiddushin*, 31a and 32a; R. Samson (Rash of Sens), *Pe'ah* I:1; Maimonides, *Hilkhot Mamrim*, 6:3.

[49]*Sifra, Kedoshim*, 86d; *Kiddushin* 30b.

Concept of Tzedakah in Contemporary Jewish Life

Leo Jung

Tzedakah as we know it today is based on the classic patterns of the Torah. It is useful to examine these roots to determine in what respects we are coming closer to the original ideas and in what manner we must still labor to reach them.

THE LOWEST FORM OF CHARITY

The sociological structure of the Jewish people is evident in the Torah's tzedakah legislation. There was a time when the Hebrew word for a merchant was "non-Jew." During that long period, Jews were either shepherds or farmers; "*Kenaani* (Canaanite)" was the technical term for merchant. The first laws dealing with palliative tzedakah indicate preoccupation with farm life. "*Leket*" (the prohibition against gleaning dropped ears of one's corn), "*shikhah*" (the instruction to take home the forgotten sheaf), "*peah*" (the obligation to leave a corner of the field unharvested), and every third year, "*ma'asser*" (the rule of contributing to the tithe of the produce for God's four protégés: the orphan, the widow, the stranger and the Levite)—all point to an agricultural society. Later on, when Jews began to be inhabitants of cities, there came two other forms—one called "*kuppah*," the charity box (the great-

96

great-grandmother of Federation) and the other, *"tamhuy,"* the food basket. But with all these forms of tzedakah the Talmud emphasized that the handout, the gift direct, is the lowest form of charity because it interferes with the self-respect of the recipient.

One rabbi in the Talmud is quoted as saying to a man who had just handed a gift to another in public: "You would have performed a much greater mitzvah had you not given it to him." And one of our earliest great scholars, Rashbo, when asked why, since before the performance of every mitzvah, *"over le-assiyatan,* we pronounce a blessing (some of you will remember it from Friday night blessing of the candles, from Shofar or Lulav), tzedakah seems to be an exception. We ought to pronounce a blessing when we give tzedakah, because it is a fundamental Biblical obligation." Said the Sage: "You dare not pronounce a blessing when you give tzedakah because every act of charity has two aspects. One is the blessing of being able to give; the other is the curse of being dependent for one's fundamental needs on the gifts of flesh and blood. And because of our brother's curse you dare not pronounce a blessing."

The palliative gift also helps only for the moment, leaving our brother as poor as he was before; it relieves very often the giver rather than the recipient, hence is the lowest form of charity.

THE RECONSTRUCTIVE WAY

The higher form of tzedakah is the free loan. Every Jewish community that considers itself to have come of age has a Hebrew Free Loan Society. What the Torah prohibits is not only usury but also the taking of any kind of financial interest. When my brother is in trouble, his emergency must not be an opportunity for me to enrich myself, but, rather, to show him brotherhood. When

I give a man a gift for his basic needs, I am affecting his self-respect. In our own national sanctuary, more than two thousand years ago, we had a special chamber, the "*Lishkat-Hashaim* (the Cell of the Silent)." Its door had a hole or slit through which those who had money could put it in; the respectable poor were encouraged to come from the other side and take what they needed. The giver would not know to whom he gave. The recipient did not know from whom he received.

But with all that, it is very sad to have to rely on others for one's vital needs and wants. That is why there is the legal obligation (not dependent on the type of breakfast we have had, the complexion of the latest Stock Exchange sheet, or the type of mood we are in) to lend to our brother in need of our ready cash. Whatever we do not absolutely need in order to obtain our own livelihood, we should lend to our neighbor whom we respect and who we know will not waste, but return it.

This second type of charity is reconstructive, because the free loan enables a man to re-establish himself, to eke out a living, to work out his economic salvation. If he is a craftsman, the free loan will enable him to buy raw materials, shape them into a marketable commodity and live on his profit. If he is a peddler, he may commence his career by seeking customers and impressing them with his reliability, thus gradually extending both the list of his goods and the scope of his terrain. This is how many of today's American millionaires started. One of the most happy aspects of American Jewish life was the work of the "*landsmanschaften*"engaged en masse in the free loan. They lent every immigrant a small sum and a basket for goods out of which developed his later affluence. But the reconstructive way of tzedakah does not solve the whole problem.

PREVENTIVE CHARITY

The boldest and most farsighted method of dealing with poverty is the preventive one. It is also one of the most difficult methods. How did the Torah describe it? When Joshua conquered the Holy Land, in accordance with the teaching of Dvarim, the fifth book of Moses, he parcelled it out to individual farmers (*Halukat Haaretz*). We learn from the Torah how it was divided. If a man wanted to use land for grazing purposes, he would get a larger tract. If he planned to engage in agriculture, he was granted a smaller one. For purposes of intensive agriculture, he received a still smaller piece (*ziborit, benonit, eedit*).

The Torah differed fundamentally from other sources in its interpretations concerning property. I have always felt that the Torah is the root of all such interpretations, in that it contains not a single law or ordinance that is accidental. All of them go back to roots, to basic concepts. The basic principle of the Torah is that the world belongs to God, that we are but trustees of its goods, and that we must make the best use of the earth and what it holds, both for ourselves and our fellow man.

This land might as well have been distributed once and for all. In every country, even in America, there are some *batlanim* (inefficient people), some sick persons, some incapable of prolonged work. These people would gradually sell their family tracts. Thus, after a time, a number of people would have been left without any acres, while others would have owned great estates. But for the Jews there was a rider attached to that law. The Torah said that: "*At no time may anyone sell his tract 'litzemitut' in perpetuity.*" In the fiftieth year, the year of Jubilee, the tract had to revert to the original family, so that no family bereft of its acreage could be absolutely poor for two generations.

If a man sold his field in accordance with the law of the Torah, he sold it on what real estate men call leasehold. That is, he gave the purchaser the right to work it for a number of years, while he received a type of rent. In the fiftieth year, he got his field back. That means that the Torah intended every family to have a source of income; and every able-bodied man to hold a job,—and, hence, some land—so that, while we might always have some poor people, we won't have hereditary pauperism.

The Torah provided that there should be no two generations of any family without a tract of land, which means a source of income or a job. Thus the Torah instituted the right to a job in its early legislation. This arrangement worked beautifully for centuries, but as people had more and more children among whom their tracts had to be divided, eventually the frontiers of ancient Palestine could not be sufficiently extended to accommodate them all. Since they had to subdivide the family field again and again for each new generation, the time eventually came when further subdivision would have been meaningless—there was simply not enough acreage for each family to derive sufficient income from the harvest. Then something uniquely Jewish happened. The people came to the Sanhedrin, the Supreme Court in Jerusalem, and they said, "We all obey the law. We all recognize it is meant to protect everyone's opportunity to earn a living. We can't subdivide our family acreage anymore. But there are our wives and children who need sustenance. What shall we do now?" The judges at the Sanhedrin studied the sacred text and made a very far-reaching decision. They said: "Back of the law of Jubilee, of the division of the land with the condition that the land must go back in the year of '50 to the original owners, is the principle, that it is the obligation of the state or society to provide every able-bodied man with a job. It is the task of the government or the Sanhedrin, its judiciary arm, to find some kind of a job for every person."

And, in fact, this decision was applied.

THE ANCIENT UNEMPLOYED

From the seventeenth volume of the *Antiquities of the Jews*, written by Joseph Flavius we take the following story:

> When the temple of Herod was finished, 1500 building workers came to the Sanhedrin. They said, "Your honors, we have been excessively praised for the work we have done (that temple was acknowledged as one of the eight world wonders) but we beg leave to say that our wives and children want to eat, even now. We have heard that the law of the Torah, the law of Jubilee in practical application means your obligation, honored Judges, as representatives of the government, to give us a job during times of depression. We have come to you and ask for your decision."

In our own country in the year 1932, there were hunger marchers going to Washington. In that case, somebody who will be nameless asked the general in charge who will also be nameless, to shoot at them. But when the building workers came to the Sanhedrin, the judges said, "You are right." They appointed a commission to determine what should be done to tide the laborers over the years of depression. They decided that, since the temple was such a magnificent and world-famous building, they ought to build an annex—to provide jobs for the 1500 building workers. But the Romans, who are great-great-grandparents of some of the administrators of the British Empire, had not forgotten what good soldiers the Jews had made. And so they said, "No. An annex to the temple means potentially another fortress! We won't permit it. No annex to the temple!" The 1500 building workers went back to the Sanhedrin and said, "Our wives and children would still like to be fed." Another commission was immediately appointed and it came up with another, more universally acceptable, solution.

At that time there was *Yerushalayim Hagdolah*, the Great Jerusalem, bigger than today's Israeli and Jordan Jerusalems together. The commission members discovered that the pavement of Great Jerusalem was in bad condition. By some lucky accident, white marble was very cheap at that time. And so, as Josephu reports in his sober prose, in order to supply jobs for the building workers, the whole of Jerusalem was paved with white marble.

In 1932 this country was in bad shape. The wheels of industry were almost at a standstill, and President Franklin Delano Roosevelt faced the crisis. He gathered together his so-called "brain-trust," and asked their advice about the amount of national debt the U.S. could stand. When he established his highly effective Public Works Administration, Roosevelt was following a precedent set in the city of Jerusalem, which in turn was based on the radical principle of the Torah that we have already discussed.

Peter Stuyvesant once established a condition for admitting Jews to New York City—a condition which we have kept religiously: that we must take care of our own poor. Stuyvesant didn't know that the Hebrew Bible has no word for "Shnorrer" ("Beggar"). The only term the Torah uses is "your Brother": "If your brother is poor, then do this or that; don't oppress him, don't oppress him with words, don't oppress him by your attitude; if you lend him money don't come to meet him in order to embarrass him." Our people have consistently honored their pledge to Peter Stuyvesant, but in a manner which he could never have imagined.

THE HIGHEST ETHICAL LEVEL

There are three Hebrew words that occur again and again in our literature: *hen, hessed* and *rahamim*. The first means "grace," the second "kindness;" the third, for the moment, I will leave untranslated. It is the highest term in Jewish ethics and one of the sweetest words in the human vocabulary.

Hen means grace—one can give aid, loan money or provide a job with grace. One can also do these things gracelessly. We have learned in the course of our historical migrations just how gracelessly "good work" can be done.

Hessed means kindness, the sort of kindness that takes into consideration the unhappiness that must be felt by the person who is to get relief. *Hessed* also includes plans of help, not for today alone, but also for the future.

But the most wonderful word, which cannot be adequately rendered in English, is *rahamim*. Usually it is translated as "pity" or "mercy." But it really means something much deeper and finer. The root of *rahamim* is "*rehem*," womb—"motherhood". "Rahamim" means mother-love, the mother's passion to spend herself, what she is, what she has, what she knows, in order to help the infant towards maturity. Until we are motivated by that type of sentiment towards everyone who is a poor brother, we will not begin to act on the Jewish level of *rahamim*. Peter Stuyvesant would have been happy if we had supplied the poor people with shelter, food and clothing. But Jewish law bids us provide him also with economic opportunity, intellectual training and emotional satisfaction.

I feel that the New York Federation combines all three aspects of tzedakah in its manifold, life and spirit-saving activities. It gives aid, in the form of the handout and the weekly check. It also provides for the various emergencies that assail its wards. But the Federation also goes beyond that; it aids people by giving them free loans and especially by providing them with a chance to earn their own living. To my mind, the rehabilitation center is the highest peak of this endeavor. The work of the Federation is a profound promise and a greater challenge to everyone. To all of us who would be proud Jews and proud Americans, the major contributions of the Jew to America are not bigger and better department stores, or bigger and better legal or medical shops—it is *"rahamanut,"* the attitude of selfless dedication to all in need, the type of tzedakah activity that comes from heart and mind, spelling out the noblest aspects of community personality. To be able to offer light to the blind, food to the hungry, encouragement to the hopeless, good cheer to the despondent— that is the highest opportunity for good men and women.

Our Jewish Poor: How Can They Be Served?

Jerome M. Comar

In recent years the collective conscience of the American Jewish community has been increasingly troubled by a growing awareness of the needs of the domestic Jewish poor, and by its own inability to deal more effectively with this problem.

We are all concerned about poverty. But we must be careful. Here in affluent America, where poverty is relatively invisible, it is easy, through constant repetition, to reduce the term to an abstraction. We must try to understand poverty in its human context. Much has been written about the state of hopelessness and despair in which the poor find themselves. Our Social Welfare and Family Agencies do much to help, but we must remember that in the final analysis the root cause, the gut issue if you will, is money.

Let's look at what it means, in money terms, to be poor in America today. The definition of poverty used by the Bureau of the Census in 1969 was an annual income of $3,743 for an urban family of four. Let me break that down a bit. This means the average income for each member of this family of four could be no more than about $935 a year, or approximately $2.57 a day. Think of that—to be considered poor by the United States government, your income cannot exceed $2.57 a day. That is less than half the price of dinner at a moderate-price restaurant.

But are you aware that being officially "poor"—even within the terms of the incredible dollars-and-cents definition I have just mentioned—is not sufficient to make you eligible for governmental aid? Figures differ from state to state, but let me give you some figures from Cook County, Illinois. The current Cook County Public Aid standard for a family of four persons (father, mother, and two children) with a maximum shelter allowance of $123.32 a month, is $282.83 a month or $3,394 a year. This is the amount which such a family would receive if it had no independent income and, of course, it is only 90.6 percent of the poverty level previously defined. Make no mistake about it, in many places in our country it is much worse. And Mississippi is not the only example—ask our colleagues from Missouri, Indiana, Maryland or Ohio about the standards of relief payments in their states. Would you believe that the average money payment under Old Age Assistance in this country is $77.30 a month? The average money payment to a needy blind person is $104. To a recipient under the Aid to Families With Dependent Children category, the monthly payment throughout the nation averages $49.35. Even with the free medical care which these programs provide, the mathematics of survival are appalling, and these are the people we are talking about when we talk about the poor.[1]

At this point in time, American Jewry is at a crossroad. We must face the hard facts of life regarding the plight of many of our fellow Jews in this country. We must ask, is there a difference in the nature of the responsibility we, as a community, have to a poverty-stricken Jew in America as opposed to a similarly unfortunate Jew abroad? Is the poor Jew in Chicago or Pittsburgh less worthy or less in need of our help than one in Kiriat Shemona, Budapest,

[1]Social Security Administration, *Social Security Bulletin* (Washington, D.C.: U.S. Government Printing Office, June 1971), pp. 1–2.

Casablanca or Riga? Can we try to do something about the problems of the "Black Panthers" of Jerusalem, and not be equally obligated to assist those American Jews who live in, or have fled from, areas dominated by the Black Panthers of our U.S. ghettos? Can we continue to justify to ourselves and others, the sending of increased sums of money raised in our cities to aid the overseas "poor Jews" without, at the same time, meeting our obligation to aid our own American Jewish poor? I'm not suggesting this is an either-or proposition. Our worldwide responsibilities show no signs of diminishing, and of course we will continue to meet these responsibilities. But, must we not find ways to meet all our responsibilities?

That the Jewish community has a special responsibility for its own needy is hardly a new idea. The specific concept of the organized Jewish community's responsibility for its poor is well documented historically. It is interesting that one of the earliest references to the Community Chest concept is noted in Abba Eban's great work, *My People: the Story of the Jews.* In it, he refers to the practice of sixteenth-century Turkish Jews who appointed collectors who went "from house to house to collect into a common chest for the poor."

This sense of responsibility was part of the American Jewish lifestyle from its earliest days as an identifiable community. Again drawing from Eban's historical work, we find that Peter Stuyvesant revoked his harsh order expelling the Jews from New Amsterdam on the condition "that the poor among them shall not become a burden to the Company or the Community but be supported by their own Nation."

We could go on and on, but the point is clear—traditionally and historically, abroad and in America, we Jews have publicly accepted a special responsibility for our poor.

Today, our Jewish community's role in regard to the general community reflects the sophisticated relationships, legislative and otherwise, which have been developed regarding the mutual responsibilities of private and governmental sectors for the care of the poor. Given the magnitude of the problem, no one would seriously suggest that the primary responsibility for the poor be removed from the government. But, if we are to be true to our tradition and our history, we must be ever alert to our own responsibilities for our own poor, and that clearly includes those poor people who live in our cities as well as those across the seas. If we are to do more than give mere lip service to a program of help for the Jewish poor, we must be prepared to answer the following questions:

—Who are the Jewish poor, and where may they be found?
—What services are available to the Jewish poor now; to what extent are they using them; and what are the gaps in these services?
—How can we, as Federations, focus our efforts on the needs of the Jewish poor?

If a Jewish Federation is to plan special programs for the poor, it is necessary to begin with some estimate of their numbers. Ideally, such an estimate should be prepared on the basis of a sample survey incorporating a sufficiently large number of Jewish poor to provide a basis for valid generalization. In many cases, costs or other considerations may make it impossible to conduct such a large-scale survey. In recent months many estimates have been made of the number of poor Jews in this country. Depending on the source and the criteria for inclusion, these figures have ranged from roughly 400,000 to one million. Unless the proportion of poverty is higher among the Jews than among any other white ethnic group in the country, then the latter estimate is incredibly high. The research department of the Jewish Federation of Metropolitan Chicago has estimated a national poor Jewish population of about 480,000 to 509,000.

For purposes of detailed planning of services to a particular Jewish poor population, general estimates as to the
total number of Jewish poor in a metropolitan area should
be supplemented whenever possible by estimates as to the
number in a particular neighborhood or community area.
Such statistical data are essential to the Federation when it
embarks upon the planning phase of services to an indigent
Jewish population. However, as it moves from a planning
to a service-giving stage, the Federation must develop
reliable procedures through which names can be substi-
tuted for numbers, and actual headcounts replace sample
surveys.

An initial source of case findings is in the caseload of
Federation agencies. Hopefully, data on the financial
situation of agency clients, particularly those at the poverty
level, will be available. If not, arrangements must be made
to obtain such information. Another source of such data
may be the case records of the public and private agencies
serving the poor in general. What I am referring to here
are primarily the public welfare agencies and special income maintenance and emergency service programs under
both public and private auspices. Obtaining appropriate
data from such agencies, however, may be quite difficult.

Where the program is focused on a relatively small
service or catchment area, it would be desirable to conduct
a house-by-house census of indigent Jews. This, of course,
can be quite expensive both in terms of money and personal
resources but, in the last analysis, it is the best way to do
the job. Finally, experience shows that no matter how
careful the case finding techniques may be, once services
are instituted, new, previously unidentified clients will
appear. Perhaps a combination of the techniques outlined above, together with the process of self-selection by
the poor who come to the agency seeking the offered
services, would provide the maximum coverage possible.

In common with the poor in general, the indigent Jew

must learn to cope with a series of large, impersonal, understaffed, underfinanced and largely inaccessible service-giving agencies. Help in this regard is often given by the Jewish Family Agency; but for the poor Jew, the problem is complicated by the fact that he is likely to be older than his non-Jewish opposite number, and is almost certain to have a growing feeling of isolation from his own community. This feeling may be compounded by a sense of true physical fear in his immediate environment. The poor Jew must cope with all of the almost insurmountable problems of the poor person in affluent America, as well as with the problems arising from his Jewishness.

If he is Orthodox, as many poor Jews are, he may find his mobility very much limited by his continuing to live in the old neighborhood near his synagogue; he may find it difficult to obtain kosher food and he may find accepting help from public or non-Jewish private agencies an affront to his dignity as a Jew.

Unfortunately, we have contributed to the plight of the poor Jew. We have a responsibility to serve the majority of the Jewish population, and in the pursuit of this responsibility we have often moved our service programs away from neighborhoods which have ceased to be "Jewish," and relocated them wherever the Jews have resettled. Volumes have been written and endless hours of debate have taken place over the wisdom of such program redirection, but that is not at issue here today. What can be said is that many service-giving agencies of the Jewish community did pursue what they felt was a right and proper course in providing service for the majority of their constituency, and in so doing further contributed to the plight of the minority. In recent years, some special programs have been developed to meet the needs of this largely abandoned population, and some Federations are beginning to refocus special programs toward this group. In the former case, the programs are often too small and reflect a particular ideological point of view which may not be acceptable to all they seek to serve. The latter programs are still, unfortunately, largely isolated and uncoordinated. At this time, Federations should be prepared to consider seriously the expenditure of major financial and other resources toward the solution of the medical, nutritional, financial and social problems of the Jewish poor, if it is found that governmental programs are inadequate.

To a great extent, the planning task facing Federation agencies today is similar to that with which our nation grappled in the 1930s. That is to say, we are in a position in which we must reflect upon basic concepts and, if indicated, be prepared to reject hallowed shibboleths. In the 1930s, it was recognized that local or private philanthropy could not adequately meet the income maintenance needs of the nation's poor. With the passage of the Social Security Act, the Federal government was cast into a new role—as the primary provider of basic financial assistance for the indigent. Most of the people involved, both lay and professional, applauded this new direction. But somewhere along the way something went wrong. The purpose of this chapter is not to discuss the public welfare system of the United States, except insofar as it specifically relates to the Jewish poor. However, certain issues are clear:

1. Public welfare has not provided the solution many expected of it.
2. Rather than diminishing, welfare rolls have grown.
3. Adequate levels of assistance have never been established.
4. The Federal welfare programs are held in generally low esteem, even by those who would ordinarily be among their most ardent supporters.
5. Programs without powerful constituencies tend to become expendable, and this should suggest to us that the outlook for meaningful welfare reform in the near future is at best less than optimistic. In the

interim, the cruel fact is that the standards of public assistance throughout the community are being cut— all this in a period of inflation and serious unemployment.

Now, where does this leave the Jewish poor? An easy answer is to say, "in the same boat as the rest of the poor— no better, no worse." However, this oversimplification in no way relieves us of our special responsibility for the Jewish poor. Partly in response to a growing awareness of the weakness of our welfare system, our government, through the efforts of several administrations, has developed a series of supplementary programs of self-help for "economically deprived minority groups." We are learning that for the purposes of much of this type of legislation, economically deprived Jews are not considered to be part of such a minority group. As a group, we have made it to the mainstream, perhaps at the expense of some of our less fortunate co-religionists. The apparent basis of this public policy is that, although some Jews may be poor, their poverty is not caused by their "Jewishness" as, for example, the poverty of blacks and Spanish-speaking minorities may be derivative of their ethnicity—an interesting proposition, although not one which we will consider here. I recognize, however, that some of our Jewish community relations organizations might interpret the situation somewhat differently.

At any rate, we must face the fact that the minimal cash needs of poor Jews are not being met by either regular welfare programs or the special programs directed to the needs of "minority groups." Unless we are prepared to accept this situation, we must be willing to question the basic tenet which has relegated the sole responsibility for financial assistance to the governmental sector. This suggestion is not made lightly. There is the issue of the philosophical anguish, the blood, the sweat and the tears expended to move our agencies beyond the level of dispensers of financial assistance to professionally-oriented treatment programs—and our agencies are among the best. There are potentially large sums of money which we may be called upon to allocate for direct assistance, particularly if supplementation means, for all practical purposes, the assumption of total financial support. We do not know the total magnitude of the cost that could be required. These issues cannot be easily resolved to everyone's satisfaction, but they must be faced within the context of the realities of the 1970s. I do not suggest that we cast aside the lessons of history. However, we must not be entrapped by the past. We must openly examine our assumptions and be prepared to make major investments of resources in creative and innovative programs to meet the needs of today.

Closely related to the above-mentioned task is one of investigation—case finding and vigilance. We simply don't know enough about the Jewish poor. We cannot be content with vague estimates, or with reliance upon service figures or data from the welfare rolls. We must go out, locate them and engage them in service programs with our affiliates. In so doing, we need not be defensive or apologetic about what we have done thus far. We have been providing services for the Jewish poor, and in large quantities. In Chicago, for example, more than 19,000 economically disadvantaged Jews received service from Jewish Federation of Metropolitan Chicago and Jewish Welfare Fund affiliates. This is not something about which we may be inordinately proud, nor does it provide laurels upon which we may comfortably rest. But it does give us a base on which we can build. And it is essential that the current planning direction now emphasized by Federations throughout the continent give high priority to the location and identification of the Jewish poor.

We must also be in the forefront of those striving for legislation and administrative regulations which maximize the opportunities for poor Jews to receive their fair share of the welfare dollar. And we should try to eliminate those practices which nullify supplementation through private philanthropy by deducting the value of such supplementation from the welfare payment. Nor must we fail to stand side by side with nonsectarian sister agencies in their effort to assist in the development of more adequate governmental welfare programs. In the 1930s, much of our Jewish leadership was in the forefront of the struggle for welfare reform— we should be there today.

Additionally, it is essential that Federations give a high priority to meeting the needs of the Jewish poor. We must use whatever leverage we have to mobilize our agencies into an intensive war against Jewish poverty. Our agencies are concerned; they want to make a greater impact on the problem. But their structure is not particularly suited to such a campaign. We tend to develop programs around functional service problems. Even such agencies as the Family Service have clearly circumscribed service boundaries. We must develop a mechanism for co-ordinating agency service so that we may focus a comprehensive program toward a microcosm of the community, initially distinguishable only by its economic deprivation. This may mean a revision of internal priorities or a delay of new programs. We cannot expect our affiliates to do this in a vacuum. What is required is coordination, community-wide vision and leadership. This, the Federation can provide.

Let us understand that this is going to cost money. Some of it may have to be absorbed through the reordering of agency priorities. It will become more incumbent than ever upon Federations to develop new sources of support, both from traditional and nontraditional areas. Although I hope the time for it will never come, it is conceivable that we may have to consider a special Jewish Poverty Emergency Fund. It is important that we deal with this problem in a deliberate and thoughtful manner. We must avoid the emotional response which in the long run helps no one, and may serve to further dash the hopes of the poor by raising false expectations. This, too, is consistent with the current planning emphasis, and does not preclude emergency responses where the conditions so indicate.

We are currently working on a number of projects of this sort in Chicago. First, as previously suggested, our agencies provide a substantial amount of service on an ongoing basis to poor Jews. Of the 70,000 Jews served during the year by Jewish Federation and Welfare Fund agencies in Chicago, we estimate that about 19,000 (27 percent) are economically disadvantaged Jews—that is, poor and near poor. This means, incidentally, that our agencies are providing direct service to 68 percent of the economically disadvantaged Jews in the area. Of course, the proportion of those Jews served by our agencies who are in fact poor, varies widely among our agencies, going from about 1 percent among the inpatients served by one of our hospitals, to around 10 percent of the Jews served in the Jewish Community Centers, 30 percent in our Family Service, 60 percent in our Vocational Service and close to 100 percent in our Homes for the Aged. It is estimated that about 25 percent of those served by our Jewish Educational Agencies receive some sort of scholarship assistance.

Since July of this year the Jewish Federation has funded, on a grant basis, a relatively small free medical-social-legal service for the indigent Jewish population of the city's Albany Park section, an area once heavily populated by middle-class Jews but now with pockets of mostly poor Jewish families and aged individuals. This religiously-oriented program, known as the Ark, although not initiated by Federation seeks, through cooperation with our agencies, to focus services on a particularly deprived segment of the Jewish population. While it offers a full range of services, it does not deal with the income maintenance problems of its client population, except for an emergency loan fund. Heavy emphasis has been placed on the use of professional and lay volunteers. Clearly, a key objective of the project is the reinforcement and re-awakening of Jewish identification and commitment, particularly among the younger volunteers. An especially gratifying development has been the enthusiasm with which our Jewish doctors and lawyers have offered their volunteer services. It is still too early to comment upon the overall effectiveness of the Ark Program, which the Federation is currently engaged in examining.

The Federation recognizes its responsibility to deal with emergency income maintenance needs of the Jewish poor, which arise as a result of temporary breakdowns in governmental services. In mid-October, when a cut-back in the General Assistance rolls was announced, the Federation swung into action to pick up the slack. Working with the Family Agency, Federation staff members took steps to identify those Jews affected. At the time this chapter was being prepared, the cutback had been delayed one month. Meanwhile, the Federation Board has granted standby authorization to meet the financial needs which might occur; and we are prepared to deal with this emergency by dispensing limited financial assistance for the balance of the year.

The planning staff of the Federation is currently developing a proposal for a short-term, action-focused planning effort involving those affiliates which serve the Jewish poor. Its objective would be to explore with greater precision the nature of the problem and its programmatic and financial implications, and to propose a specific program of action for dealing with it. As proposed, the planning effort would fully explore the implications and feasibility of Federation involvement in an ongoing program of financial assistance to the Jewish poor.

We must face the reality of change. The welfare system, as we have known it since its inception in the 1930s, is under-

going a period of transformation—and we must recognize
that the transformation of any system brings with it periods
of uncertainty. Such periods provoke crisis; and, if there
are times when governmental funds are not available, we
must be prepared—within the limit of our ability to do so,
and, of course, within the limits of governmental guidelines—to step in and supplement the system for Jews in
need of help. We must do this at least until such time as
our welfare system is transformed into a workable, fiscal-
ly sound system which serves the poor and disadvantaged
adequately.

The steps I have described are a beginning, and we believe they are worthy of consideration. As a community we
Jews must act on behalf of the Jewish poor—"If not now,
when?"

Problems in Serving Chicago's Jewish Poor

Aviva Silberman

The basic problem in delivering adequate services to the Jewish poor is that so many people are either unaware, or unwilling to accept the harsh reality of Jewish poverty. Until we teach our own people that there are persons of widely different socioeconomic statuses within what is generally considered an upper-middle-class ethnic group, and help them to understand what being a poor Jew is all about, we will be unable to provide the variety of services needed to help the elderly Jewish poor live out their lives in greater comfort and the younger generation to escape from the cycle of poverty.

The figures recently released by Chicago's Jewish Federation, which state that there are 18,000 poor Jews and 8,500 near poor Jews in the metropolitan area, are probably not precise. In any case, they do not exaggerate the seriousness of the situation for the particular families involved and the Jewish community in general. Unfortunately, some people have taken this report as a reason for not doing anything—since the numbers are so large—while others consider it "just another gimmick" for raising funds. Until we put our own house in order we will not be able to exert the force necessary to insure that the Jewish community receives its share of the governmental funds designated for services to the disadvantaged.

The Jewish community cannot assume that, because

the city's poverty program operates in some communities, it is reaching poor Jews. Past conversations with the poverty agency's staff indicate that they are not cognizant of the poor Jews in their midst. They have recognized that some elderly Jews come to their seniors' programs, but they regard them as different from the other elderly people who come there. Even professional staff members, including some Jews, have believed so strongly in the stereotype of the middle-class Jew that they assumed these individuals had adequate savings and family to fall back upon. Two meetings were held with the subprofessional staff of the Montrose Urban Progress Center, the last in the winter of 1969. The purpose of these informal gatherings was to try and secure from the staff members the names of Jewish poor people in the area with whom they had come into contact. Not one such name was available, and considerable surprise was registered regarding the topic of conversation. From the discussion it became clear that when the Community Representatives (CRs) came into a building and saw a Jewish name on the bell, they did not attempt to make contact with that household. Three basic reasons for this were given:

—The CRs believed that they would be unable to talk to the resident, partly because they thought the person would not speak English and partly because they felt they would be unable to relate to a Jewish household. They emphasized that people were best served when they dealt with persons of their own background.

—Some CRs spoke rather vaguely of another sort of response, somewhat related to the first, which indicated a certain amount of prejudice towards Jews.

—However, by far the most frequent reason given was that the CR was sure the family living in the apartment, being Jewish, couldn't be poor. Indeed, several workers suggested that the Jewish families must own the building.

The Jewish poor are not represented on poverty program boards. These boards have included some individuals of the Jewish faith, on the citywide committee and within the local advisory council in the Uptown area. And membership of a rabbi from the periphery of the poor Jewish community within the Montrose Urban Progress Center council may have been considered as official representation from that community. But even during periods that emphasized self-representation by the poor, there was none on that board who came from the Jewish poverty population, or who had a specific relationship to it.

At the citywide level, the original board appointed in 1964 had no official representation from the Jewish community. Sometime during late 1965 or early 1966 the executive director of the Chicago Board of Rabbis was appointed to that group. However, an examination of membership lists issued in October 1968, and May 1969, indicate that he had been dropped from the group during a reorganization process.

This gentleman's name reappeared on the October 1970 list, and remained on the list issued in January 1971. But at no time was the Jewish Federation, one of its constituent agencies, or any other Jewish lay organization on the committee, nor was membership sought. Despite the fact that at one time (the fall of 1967) as many as ten individuals of the Jewish faith sat on the poverty board, nobody spoke for the Jewish poor, suggested that the program should also address their needs, or felt it was important that a poor Jew be among the poverty population represented on that committee.

In the same manner, no one group has taken the responsibility for calling the problems of a Friday afternoon and evening food stamp registration program for non-aid recipients to the attention of the county; nor has any group worked toward changes in administrative regulations and laws governing supplemental aid for the purposes of maintaining *kashruth*. While the total community must be concerned with the Jewish poor, one particular group must become responsible, not for representing them, but for working with them to insure that their interests are represented at all levels within the Jewish and general communities.

Since the organizations and individuals in authority have accepted the idea that the Jewish community is a middle-class community, a considerable amount of all programming is cast in a middle-class mold. Thus, a mother who has no understanding of the ways of psychological counseling can only express anger and frustration when her teenager's counselor quite properly refuses to share certain confidential information with her:

> We were all invited in to see how we relate . . . he (the counselor) just sat and rocked back and forth, smoked his pipe. I kept asking what I could do to help and he was silent.

The interviewer reported that he had taken the mother's understanding of the nature of the counseling situation for granted, and that he had also suggested counseling for her, but she was so angered by what she felt was the counselor's "sneering" attitude that she refused to return. A middle-class mother might well have been assured by the counselor's professional manner, but in a family where four people live on less than $5,000 a year in a crowded, deteriorating apartment, it is not surprising to find a very different response.

Perhaps a major reason for the middle-class approach of the agencies within the Jewish community is that the governing boards of practically every community organization consist of upper and upper-middle-class individuals, and in the case of some bodies a considerable number of the "leaders," in terms of voting board membership, come from the periphery of the Jewish community. The selection of top staff members, the subsequent choice of their subordinates, and the development of programs tend to reflect the background and outlook of these boards. Though some community boards may be especially top heavy with older, wealthy, and/or assimilated individuals, virtually all Jewish organizational boards reflect this problem to some extent.

The Jewish community and its institutions must be democratized. Members must be chosen on the basis of their commitment to the continuation of the Jewish way of life, with some knowledge of the faith, and from as many different backgrounds as possible in terms of affiliation with each of the branches of Judaism and socioeconomic status. All age groups must also be adequately represented.

A report to the Board of Directors of the Jewish Federation dated April 26, 1971 notes that "about 50% of our clients are in the poor category." How many of these individuals, or people of like backgrounds, have been suggested for membership on the various agency boards? There is leadership potential within the Jewish poverty community, despite the many problems found there, and the total community must assist in locating and developing these individuals. The needs of the poor Jews, who make up such a large percentage of the Jewish welfare agencies's caseload, can be best met if their representatives have the opportunity to determine and interpret their needs to the total community, as equal participants. It is not suggested that 50 percent of all boards be made up of the poor, but there must be a total opening up of the community's organizational structures to the whole community, including the poor. Hopefully, this development would also lead to the introduction and training of paraprofessional human service workers within the Jewish community.

Only through a democratization of the structures of Jewish communal life will the community be able to maintain itself as a creative, viable entity. With input from a greater variety of backgrounds, our agencies will be able to define their work in terms of the needs of all the Jewish people in the community, hopefully becoming more successful in reaching and serving them. Finally, staff members will become more aware of their need to maintain a position of accountability and relevance to the total community.

When a middle-class person needs help, he generally knows where to go and how to find the assistance he needs. He may have some initial reluctance in seeking help, depending upon his problem and his age, but in general he is ultimately able to connect with a service source. On the other hand, the people under study for this chapter were not overly aware of helping agencies and had little contact with them. This is characteristic of all poverty populations.

People living in poverty will seldom go outside of a small geographic area for services, since they may not know where or how to look for the assistance they need. They may exhibit great reluctance in going outside of their own community, often because of lack of carfare, baby sitter funds, or proper clothing. They tend to personify sources of assistance and to seek out people who are familiar to them and with whom they feel comfortable. The introduction of a variety of neighborhood-based services into a poverty community is one way of helping individuals, families and local institutions participate actively in area problem-solving.

Such programs would help the Jews of Albany Park, the area of Chicago which seems to have the greatest concentration of Jewish poverty. Governmental programs have tended to concentrated on the areas of greatest poverty, and since the poverty area of Albany Park represents a small pocket within a working-class area, bounded on three sides by wealthier neighborhoods, little attention has been paid to its problems. Furthermore, a considerable number of poor Jews are scattered throughout a variety of nonpoverty areas, often renting the least desirable apartments (over stores, in basements) in such neighborhoods as North Park and West Ridge. Thus, neighborhood-based services and governmental action alone are not the total answer, but both must play a role in any plan the Jewish community develops to meet this problem.

Mrs. K., an American-born, 57-year-old factory worker, is one example of a typical member of the Jewish poverty community. As with so many other Chicagoans, the factory in which she worked has moved to the suburbs. This has created a crisis in the K's four-room, one bedroom apartment, where Mrs. K. is the basic support of her 53-year-old invalid husband, her 27-year-old daughter and son-in-law, both of whom have only been able to secure part-time factory work, and her six-year-old granddaughter. Currently they are living on income Mr. K. receives from Social Security (a disability pension), and the earnings of the children—a total of about $3,500 annually. The apartment is described as "poorly furnished, but very clean" and Mrs. K. as "not synagogue oriented, but very aware of being Jewish."

She has been looking for employment by visiting factory areas known to her. Though she had heard of JVS (the Jewish Vocational Service), she was totally reluctant to visit the Devon Avenue office, saying that the area was "not for her." She told the interviewer that it was an area for "rich Jews" and no amount of urging could convince her otherwise. With the train to 1 South Franklin [the Chicago Jewish Federation Building] almost at her door the interviewer tried that approach, but again the woman spoke of the difficulty of the "L" steps downtown and her great reluctance to go to an unfamiliar area.

Of course, there is no guarantee that Mrs. K. would have gone to a neighborhood center on her own had one been present, but her opportunities for obtaining service in a manner she would find comfortable would have been greatly increased. A second example illustrates the problems of a poor Jew in finding the right agency to serve her.

Mrs. R. is European-born, a post-World War II immigrant, 44 years old, and a widow with two young children to support. She has no skills. She went to the JVS office on Devon and from there was referred to the Montrose Urban Progress Center. Though at that time her only source of income was Social Security, based upon her husband's earnings, she claims that the Center staff was at first reluctant to talk to her because she lived in a nonpoverty area.

According to Mrs. R., after talking to her they told her they couldn't refer her for employment unless she took their Urban Living classes. She was admittedly not anxious to do that, as it would mean spending money on carfare and a sitter for her children, as well as going far from home at night, into what she considered a dangerous area. She reports that she was told that the course was about life in the city and how to adjust to it, plus learning how to read and write. She felt that she didn't need that. Mrs. R. told the interviewer that she was literate. Her English, though heavily accented, is very understandable, and quite grammatical, considering that it is not her primary language. Though her schooling had been interrupted in the tenth grade, while she was in a concentration camp, she had gone to school after coming to the United States, and had passed the citizenship test.

Mrs. R. reports that the counselor then told her that it was just as well that she wasn't anxious to take the classes, because they were going to recommend that she not come back for them, as she wouldn't fit in with the group—they might not like her being there. However, she insists that they told her that without the classes they could do nothing for her and suggested she get "some Jewish people" to help her or go to a Jewish agency. Though Mrs. R. sought out other forms of service, the services presently available did not meet her needs.

One of the things that ought to be explored in attempting to expand services to the Jewish poor is the feasibility of active outreach and casefinding. The report of the Gerontological Council of the Jewish Federation notes the frequent need for this among the elderly; it may also be a need among the younger poor.

Indeed, the whole outreach concept is one that, not only Jewish social service agencies, but also the synagogues, will have to grapple with. How much of the community's general lack of outreach is based upon Judaism as a non-proselytizing faith, and how much of it is based upon the roots of American Judaism in the European *shtetl*, where everybody knew everybody else and their problems? How much of it is a desire for privacy stemming from this background? This is difficult to say but, in any case, modern-day America is not the European shtetl, and it will be necessary for all groups within the community to rethink their approach in terms of actively reaching out to the poor Jews within their midst.

According to the interviews held with local clients, it appears that the services rendered by our Jewish agencies are frequently crisis-oriented and single-issue in nature.

—Mr. S. reports that, though the counseling received by his family relative to a change in family roles due to his illness and severely reduced income was most satisfactory, his requests for help with his boys's education were not followed up.

—Mrs. R. reports a referral for her own job needs, but no interest in following up on needs she expressed for school and job counseling for her handicapped daughter.

—Mr. T. expresses a positive reaction to the personal counseling he is receiving, but unhappiness that requests to the counselor for information on out-of-city schools that might accept him, scholarships and draft counseling have not been met.

—Mr. K. came to the agency with a variety of legal, financial and emotional problems, including a youngster who had been involved with the police—and insists that the worker was only willing to deal with one situation, and that through a referral to a public agency for whose services he was ineligible.

It may well be that the additional service requested in each of these cases had to come from a different source, but that can present a very real problem to the poor individual. There is a great need for total service programming. Not only must the agency view the person served as a total human being, but the manner in which service is given must help that person view the agency and its parts as a whole. Anything else leads to fragmentation of service and what may seem like orderly steps in receiving help to the middle-class individual will be viewed as a hopeless maze by the poor.

The suggestions in the Gerontological Council's report apply just as well to the problems of the Jewish poor as to programs for the elderly.

While many individual institutional programs can be singled out as valuable, the system within which they are delivered, as it exists in this community today, is generally considered outmoded and inconsistent with current thinking.

This study has raised some unanswered questions to which the community should direct its attention. For example, what role does Jewish identity play in counseling and other services that Jewish agencies provide to Jews? What, if anything, is done within Jewish social service agencies that makes their programming different from that found in general community agencies? (These questions apply to service given to all Jews, regardless of socioeconomic background.) In terms of counseling provided to poor Jews, are both the religious and the financial factors in the individual's life considered? To what extent is Jewish identity an aid in the recovery of the emotionally disturbed individual, rich or poor? Have Jewish community agencies attempted to define what the Jewish way of providing service is, and how Jewish agencies do or should differ from other community agencies? No one is suggesting that Jewish agencies "force feed" Judaism to unwilling people. But a Jewish agency must operate with regard for the legitimate Jewish values of its clients.

Thus, when a family needs emergency foster care, but cannot receive a guarantee that their children will be placed in a Jewish environment, they tend to lose confidence in the Jewish agency with which they are dealing. When a homemaker is placed in a Jewish home, and the mother is assured that she has been trained in the regulations of maintaining a Jewish home, it is disturbing to find her washing dishes with Ivory soap. It is even more upsetting when the luncheon "treat" purchased for the children turns out to contain veal and pork, and the homemaker reacts to the mother's distress by telling her "what she thought of keeping kosher." These are just a few of the problems families interviewed reported having with Jewish agency services.

The community must also become concerned with agencies that call themselves Jewish, but maintain a nonsectarian program stance, instructing staff members to introduce no religious programming—Jewish or Christian—though allowing them to respond to requests from the youngsters for holiday observances. It should be obvious why such organizations have so much difficulty reaching the remaining Jewish youths in their area, the majority of whom are from observant homes.

The following are a few of the many ways the Jewish component can be integrated into services for all economic groups:

1. As part of the total approach to a family's needs

arrangements can be made for the children's attendance at religious school, and opportunities for
adult Jewish education can be presented to parents.
When counselors suggest that families and individuals develop outside interests, appropriate Jewish
programming might be suggested.

2. In discussing the ways in which family life can be
   strengthened and reinforced, families can be given
   information and suggestions about Jewish holidays,
   customs and ceremonies, including the opportunity
   to participate in discussion groups. A simple way
   of doing this is to discuss the value of observing the
   Shabbat in the home in a form which is meaningful
   to the particular family involved.

3. Staff and lay leadership must be knowledgeable
   about the total Jewish community and should be
   well versed in Jewish practice. Often a non-Jewish
   social service worker is unable to receive accurate
   information on something of a specifically Jewish
   nature for a family he is serving, because the staff of
   Jewish agencies only know the resources of their
   own agency.

A simple directory should be developed and widely
distributed within the Jewish community and to those
individuals and agencies in the general community who
might find it useful, providing information on the proper
authorities to contact for a variety of Jewish services and
information. This would be helpful to all Jews, and
particularly important for the poor Jew, who often lacks
knowledge and finds himself referred to a staff member of
either a Jewish or a general agency who is also uninformed.
For example, in this directory information on *Brit Milah*,—
not the regulations, but who to contact to arrange for a
Brit—would be cross-filed under "Naming a Baby." There
would be a listing of schools and suggestions on where to
call to arrange for special group programs in the area of

Jewish education and Judaica, possibly with sub-categories for the latter. Resources for information on kashruth, funerals and conversions could be included, as well as a section dealing with nursery schools and camping, plus a variety of other topics.

Finally, in discussing how a Jewish agency can reach its goals, we must confront the highly sensitive subject of open hiring policies. It would be impossible to be a Jew and not believe that such policies are good and proper. Yet, we must also be aware that they can cause a paradox within our agencies. Jewish agencies serving Jewish clients must be able to deal with problems in a Jewish way. Many times non-Jewish staff members simply cannot do this, though, of course, not all Jewish staff members can do so either. Such a situation recently came to a head in a Jewish helping agency, where the former Jewish executive, known to be antagonistic to things Jewish, retired, and was succeeded by a Christian psychiatric caseworker who is attempting to introduce Jewish content through educational programs and camping experiences.

When staff members, no matter what their background, cannot adequately serve the needs of Jewish clients, which is the supposed goal of all our organizations, they do not belong in their jobs. We must also be aware of the fact that many Jews, especially the poor Jews covered by this study, still remain uncomfortable in the presence of gentiles, since few of them have had the opportunity to know any non-Jews as individuals, or as friends. A client's inability to relate to a counselor, particularly in times of crisis or in dealing with highly personal matters, often prevents successful problem-solving. The client's problem in dealing with his counselor may be due to latent prejudice or lack of contact, with another religious group, but when a person needs help he needs help, not a lesson in inter-group relations.

The upper-class Establishment must understand that

their experiences with the gentile world may be considerably different from those of the poor Jew of Albany Park, or even the middle and working-class Jews of West Ridge and Skokie. Staffing patterns and individual assignments to clients must be reviewed so that the agency's primary function is not inhibited. In-service training must be required of all staff members to make them more aware of the community they are working for, its traditions and values.

3. THE JEWISH POOR AND THE WAR AGAINST POVERTY

Why Jews Get Less: A Study of Jewish Participation in the Poverty Program

Naomi Levine and
Martin Hochbaum

Although it has been nine years since the passage of the Economic Opportunity Act (EOA), by and large the war against Jewish poverty has not yet begun. This study is an attempt to determine why Jewish participation in the poverty program, with special emphasis on New York City, has been so minimal.

To many people the phrase "the Jewish poor" is a contradiction in terms. Jews are simply not regarded as poor. One active participant in New York City's poverty program has observed that Jews are always perceived as having money hidden away, and that the poorest among them are viewed as having secret sources of income. Even a cursory examination of the lifestyle and living conditions of thousands of Jews in the old Jewish neighborhoods of inner cities reveals the fallacy of that view.

A basic problem in discussing the Jewish poor in New York City, as elsewhere, is the lack of available demographic data. Government departments do not keep a separate listing of Jewish poor. Poverty statistics are broken down into black, Puerto Rican, and "others." The latter term includes, besides Jews, Italians, Poles, Greeks, etc. For example, while we know that in 1965 Community Corporation areas in the Borough of Manhattan had 186,382 Puerto Ricans and 383,547 Blacks, we do not have even an estimate of the number of Jews who were included in the "white" category totalling 546,396 persons.

To some extent, this lack of data is overcome by Ann G. Wolfe's study, "The Invisible Jewish Poor" included in this book. On the basis of an examination of numerous surveys and statistics gathered over a period of years, Mrs. Wolfe concludes that nearly one million Jews in the United States live at the poverty or near-poverty level, with 250,000 New York City Jews earning less than $3,000 per year.

According to this study, 60 to 65 percent of all Jewish poor are over 60 years of age. This is in contrast to the general population, where approximately 75 percent of the impoverished are under 60 years of age. The remaining one third of the Jewish poor are single individuals, families with children and families with only one parent. Members of both groups often find themselves living within a hostile environment. The major differences between these two groups of poor Jews are in the area of need. While both groups need better housing, health care, and numerous other services, the younger impoverished Jews need more education, manpower training programs and job referrals.

According to an Office of Economic Opportunity (OEO) study that follows this selection ("Jewish Participation in New York City's Poverty Program"), there is evidence of limited participation of the Jewish poor in New York City's poverty program. The reasons for this, both in New York City and elsewhere, are complex. It will be easier to understand them if they are separated into two categories, those outside the Jewish community and those within it.

Reasons outside the Jewish community. The major reason for the low participation of Jews in New York City's poverty program is that the treatment of poverty is essentially limited to certain areas of the city. (This approach is derived from the wording and emphasis of the Economic Opportunity Act and the federal guidelines used to implement that Act.) Instead of a system of citywide poverty programs which would treat poverty wherever it is found, New York City's program, taking its cue from the Economic Opportunity Act itself, is decentralized into a system of 26 poverty areas, each administered by a Community Corporation and controlled by a locally elected board of directors responsible for programs in their respective areas. Although the OEO Report lists 140,000 poor Jews living in poverty areas, many poor Jews live outside of such areas. And, while the city's Council Against Poverty could create citywide projects to cover persons living outside the poverty areas, it has embarked upon only a few such programs. This is acknowledged in a September 1971 study by the New York City Human Resources Administration entitled "Report of Findings."

The Puerto Rican Community Development Project, which is concerned with the needs of the city's Puerto Ricans wherever they may live, is a good example of one of the few citywide projects funded by the Council Against Poverty. If more such programs were funded, the Jewish poor could participate more effectively in the antipoverty program.

Where Jews live within poverty areas, their numerical weakness tends to result in their being ignored. To a great extent each poverty board is viewed as serving, not an area, but one or more specific groups within the population. Programs tend to be set up accordingly. Groups such as the Jews, who lack an effective voice on nearly all local boards, get little or nothing. Thus, while comprising perhaps 15 percent of the city's poor, Jews receive far less than their proportional share in poverty assistance.

Theoretically, the city's poverty program recognizes the existence of "pockets of poverty" outside the 26 designated poverty areas. In fact, the Council Against

Poverty has stated, in an official document entitled "New York City Poverty Area Maps" (1967):

> The Council recognizes the hardship to isolated poor persons or families who happen to reside outside of designated poverty areas. . . . The Council has made it clear . . . that needy residents in "pockets of poverty" may be served by community corporations. . . . Residents of these "pockets" are also eligible for appointment to community corporation boards.

Despite this statement, however, for all practical purposes the poor who reside outside the poverty areas have been excluded from participating in the city's poverty program. The Community Corporations do not attempt to reach out and serve these people, most of whom are unaware of the potential benefits the poverty program can provide.

The nature of the programs carried out under the Economic Opportunity Act also limits Jewish participation. Most of the Jewish poor are aged. However, there are few programs explicitly designed to meet the needs of the aged. On the national level, in 1971–72 Congress allocated only $8 million for the "Senior Opportunities and Services" program in Sec. 222 (7). In New York City, less than one percent of the money funneled through the New York City Council Against Poverty has been devoted to senior citizen programs. While the needs of the aged are increasingly acknowledged by Congress, by the Office of Economic Opportunity and by community action agencies, most such bodies—including the Council Against Poverty—do not treat the needs of the aged as a high priority item. Instead, less than $100,000 of the Council's community action funds are concerned with helping what the Office of Economic Opportunity now refers to as "older persons," despite the fact that the Economic Opportunity Act has several sections underscoring the need for programming in this field. For example, in

Title I, part B, Work and Training Programs for Youth
and Adults, there is a section which states:

> The director shall provide that programs under this part
> shall be designed to deal with the incidence of long-term
> unemployment among persons 55 years and older. In the
> conduct of such programs, the director shall encourage the
> employment of such persons as regular, part-time and short-
> term staff in component programs.

But this has seldom been done. And again, in the section
on funding the Community Action Programs, there is
the following provision:

> The director may provide financial assistance to the community
> action agencies for the planning, conduct, administration
> and evaluation of community action programs and com-
> ponents. These components may involve, without limitation,
> other activities and supporting facilities designed to assist
> participants, including the elderly poor, to secure and retain
> employment . . . make better use of income . . . to provide
> and maintain adequate housing. . . (Sec. 221)

While the failure to properly implement these mandates
has limited Jewish participation, the recently approved
EOA Extension contained an amendment by Congressman
Scheuer which, if enacted, would have better enabled
the Jewish and other unserved poor to participate in the
poverty program. This amendment authorized the spending of $50,000,000 to help those (with special emphasis
on the aged) not being served by existing programs.*
A similar amendment was introduced by Senators Harrison
Williams of New Jersey and Jacob Javits of New York.

Another reason for low Jewish participation is the fact
that many of those charged with operating poverty pro-

---

* While the idea behind this amendment was adopted, money
was never appropriated for it.

grams are simply insensitive to the needs of the Jewish poor. For example, the OEO report notes that:

> The fact that these folk (Jews living in the Brownsville, Morrisania, and Lower East Side communities) are invisible to the area poverty staff gives credence to (the) allegation that Jews are underserved.

This is not to suggest that poverty officials are anti-Semitic, but rather that they are unaware of Jewish and other white poverty, and that they are more interested in serving "their own."

Another example of this insensitivity to Jewish needs is the American Jewish Congress's experience with a questionnaire sent to the executive directors of 25 of the city's Community Corporations. In a covering letter, the organization's spokesman explained that it was conducting an examination of Jewish participation in the city's poverty program, and that it needed such information as the number of Jews on the board of directors, the area's population, the Corporation's program, etc. After a mailing and a followup contact, only four replies were received (less than one sixth of the total), including one that was so obviously inaccurate as to be useless.

The fact that most communities hold elections for the board of directors of Community Corporations on the Jewish sabbath also makes it difficult for many Jews to participate. For example, the Rockaways section of Queens, which has a Jewish population of over 70 percent, holds its election for the members of the board of directors on Saturday. In New York State this will no longer occur, because of city and state legislation enacted in 1972 that prohibits the holding of such elections on Saturday. However, much of the damage caused by sabbath elections cannot be undone because the Orthodox Jewish poor in many areas are now in the position where other local groups were in 1966. Whether or not they can "catch up" remains to be seen.

Another factor which has limited the participation of Jews in poverty area elections is the fear of physical abuse. Threats reported in the Crown Heights area of Brooklyn, when the Corporation was just getting under way, served to inhibit Jews from taking part in antipoverty elections and projects.

Still another factor that should be mentioned is the criteria used to determine a poverty area's boundaries and allocations. This not only limits Jewish participation, but also the allocation to a poverty area with Jewish residents. According to Council Against Poverty documents, the three major indices used to decide how much money each poverty area should receive are: welfare population; number of live births in city hospital wards per 100 population; and juvenile delinquency per 100 juveniles between the ages of seven and 20. Because many poor Jews are reluctant to seek public welfare assistance and because most of the Jewish poor are aged persons, none of these three criteria defines Jewish poverty. The OEO report observes that the "group characteristics (of the Jewish poor) do not relate to the indices originally used by the Poverty Council to determine target areas." This is also acknowledged in the Human Resources Administration's study.

Reasons within the Jewish community. Jewish community organizations are not blameless for the failure of the Jewish poor to take advantage of the potential benefits that are to be found in the poverty program. This situation may be attributed to a number of factors. Until recently, Jewish organizations have not generally pushed for increased participation of the Jewish population in the poverty program. The reason behind this might well be that the poverty program is frequently viewed as a program that "belongs" to blacks and Puerto Ricans. There is a belief among many people in New York City and in other urban centers—including poverty workers and poverty officers at the highest levels—that the poverty program exists to serve the needs of black and Puerto Rican citizens.

The structure of Jewish life has been another deterrent to Jewish participation in the city's poverty program. The Jewish community is well organized, but on a citywide rather than a local basis. Under the existing structure, successful participation in the poverty program requires organization on a local or community basis. It requires people in the community who are willing and able to make demands on the Community Corporations on behalf of the Jewish poor. On a neighborhood level, the Jewish community is usually not organized to exert such pressure.

Jewish involvement in the poverty program is also hampered by the feeling on the part of many Jews, especially the aged, that poverty is simply a burden that one accepts. Having internalized such values as individualism and achievement, they have a psychological roadblock to changing the conditions under which they live. Their traditional reluctance to become involved in "welfare programs" is carried over to the poverty program.

Also hindering Jewish involvement is the fact that the aged make up nearly two thirds of the Jewish poor. These people are unorganized and unable to exert influence aimed at benefiting themselves. Loneliness, fear, fatigue and other physical, economic and social problems are not conducive to seeking aid from programs aimed at treating these very ills.

Related to these disabilities is the fact that Jews in general have been unable or reluctant to engage in the "politics of poverty," which has often taken the form of the "politics of confrontation." The Human Resources Administration's "Report of Findings," for example, notes that the Council Against Poverty responds to pressure. A key demonstration every now and then, sparked with loud and vituperative demands, can go a long way toward making the city's "poverticians" aware of the plight of the poor. The traditional Jewish abhorrence of violence and of confrontation as a political weapon has discouraged similar demands by Jewish groups.

Another reason for the failure of the Jewish community to participate in the poverty program was the initial reluctance of the established Jewish social welfare organizations to get involved in the poverty program. Originally, they viewed the program as a threat to their dominance in the social welfare field. By the time they overcame this reluctance, it was too late to play more than a minor role. As a result, they have not pushed for senior citizen's programs, demanded more representation on the Council Against Poverty, submitted projects to be funded, pushed for more citywide programs, or played a role in organizing the Jewish community on a local level.

We believe that the time has come to make substantial changes in New York City's antipoverty program, and in the Jewish response to it. Only through fundamental changes in the administration and operation of the antipoverty program can the money allocated to alleviate poverty under the Economic Opportunity Act be distributed more equitably. While our suggestions are directed to New York City and our immediate concern is the Jewish poor, we believe these recommendations are applicable to other major cities and, if adopted, will benefit all of this nation's poor.

To achieve these aims, we urge that the following actions be taken:

1. The Economic Opportunity Act of 1964 should be amended.
2. Changes should be made in the administration of New York City's antipoverty program as outlined below.
3. More funds should be granted to senior citizens'

programs, and greater concern for the aged should be demonstrated by antipoverty officials.

4. More citywide programs should be funded by the Council Against Poverty, and Jewish organizations should make a concerted effort to submit plans for such citywide programs.

5. An effective citywide Jewish antipoverty organization should be created, together with local neighborhood coordinating councils, to increase Jewish participation on a citywide basis and on the local level in the existing antipoverty programs.

Changes in the Economic Opportunity Act. The very language and emphasis of the Economic Opportunity Act minimize and often exclude Jewish participation. While we cannot go into a section-by-section analysis of the Economic Opportunity Act here, we believe that it must be amended to allow the poor who do not reside in defined poverty areas to participate in poverty programs. Furthermore, federal funding for the elderly must be significantly expanded beyond the current annual allocation of $1 per elderly poor person. The amendments to the Economic Opportunity Act Extension discussed above would help meet these goals.

Changes in the administration of the antipoverty program in New York City. The composition of the New York City Council Against Poverty should be changed to assure greater representation of the Jewish community. One suggestion is to apply to the citywide Council Against Poverty the Racial and Ethnic Balance Plan adopted by the Council in July 1968, to assure greater balance on the boards of directors of local Community Corporations. Indeed, the federal government itself has directed that each community action program establish a plan for insuring equitable representation on the local board of directors among the various ethnic groups living within the areas governed by these boards. If this is needed on a local level, it is equally important to apply it to the citywide body.

The Racial and Ethnic Balance Plan must be implemented by the neighborhood corporations. Our research indicates that this plan has not been implemented, and that Jews are still inadequately represented on the boards of directors of the neighborhood corporations. For example, the OEO Report shows that, while Jews make up 72 percent of the poor in Rockaway, the board of directors of that area's Community Corporation does not have a single Jewish member. As long as this situation continues to exist, Rockaway's Jewish poor will not be treated fairly in the funding of programs and in the allocation of monies.

For the first time now, every poor Jew, regardless of the area in which he resides, must be allowed to vote for representatives to the local poverty corporations on a day other than Saturday.* In the past, the holding of these elections on Saturday in most areas in New York City violated the rights of Orthodox Jews.

Election areas must receive adequate police protection so that there is no intimidation of voters.

The criteria for choosing poverty area boundaries and allocations should be re-evaluated. Any formula that gives overriding weight to the number of welfare recipients, the number of live births in city hospitals, and the rate of juvenile delinquency is unfair to those poor communities whose inhabitants are reluctant to accept welfare, have few juvenile delinquents, and are past the age of childbearing. The overriding factor should be income level.

When all the data of the 1970 census are released, there will be a redrawing of Community Corporation boundaries. This will provide an excellent opportunity for the Jewish

---

* The 1972 Economic Opportunity Act's Extension prohibited sabbath elections.

community to demand a re-evaluation of the criteria currently being used, and to make certain that the boundaries are drawn in a manner that will benefit the Jewish poor. In some sections of New York City—the Tremont area in the Bronx, for example—many poor Jews live just outside the boundaries of the local poverty area. As a result, today they cannot participate in the programs organized by the Tremont Community Corporation. By having the boundaries changed only slightly, this group of Jews could participate in antipoverty programs.

Poverty officials at every level must become sensitive to the problems of the Jewish poor. Current attitudes of indifference to the fact of Jewish poverty are a major factor in the lack of Jewish participation in the poverty program.

More funding must be granted to senior citizen programming. Senior citizen programs have been seriously neglected in the administration of the antipoverty program. On the federal level, only small amounts of funding have been made available. On the city level the picture is even worse. An examination of existing programs indicates that in New York City only seven of the more than 250 delegate agencies are concerned with the aged poor. These agencies spend less than $500,000 annually—equal to three quarters of 1 percent of the money funneled through the New York City Council Against Poverty. The Council Against Poverty and the local community must begin to give such projects the priority they deserve.

More citywide programs must be funded by the Council .Against Poverty. The Council has the authority to fund such projects. To date, however, it has only made limited use of this power. Yet the use of such programs, as the Human Resources Administration's "Report of Findings" acknowledges is one of the most effective ways of dealing with poor persons living outside of the officially designated poverty areas.

A citywide antipoverty organization or coordinating council should be created. In New York City, the major Jewish organizations have organized such a Council. It will be responsible for maintaining current data concerning the Jewish poor; stimulating awareness in the Jewish community of programs aimed at dealing with poverty; educating Jews as to their rights and opportunities under existing programs; organizing Jews to press for programs of concern to them; working toward increasing Jewish representation on the local corporations and on the citywide Council Against Poverty; encouraging the adoption of citywide poverty programs; and working toward changing the language of the current Economic Opportunity Act so that all of the poor can benefit from it.

In sum, a citywide Jewish antipoverty council would coordinate the efforts of the Jewish community, both on a citywide basis and neighborhood by neighborhood, so that the war on Jewish poverty could finally begin.

Memorandum of Inspection Division
Office of Economic Opportunity

During our survey of Jewish participation in the New York City poverty program, staff members in four of the 25 area corporations (Crown Heights, Mid-West Side, Lower East Side, South Jamaica) were unable or unwilling to provide an estimate of the ethnic breakdown of their program participants.

In more than one case, management of the area corporations excused their lack of knowledge by explaining that they did not get any reports from their delegate agencies, that these reports go directly to the Community Development Agency (CDA). If this is true, how can they discharge the critical function of programmatic and administrative oversight, normally the key part of any prime-delegate agency relationship.

Furthermore, when questioned, the assistant deputy commissioner of CDA stated: "CDA does not require the corporations to submit a statistical record of the participants served."

It is difficult to comprehend how these corporations can select appropriate programs for their areas or adequately administer poverty programs without a comprehensive knowledge and understanding of the beneficiaries of their services.

BACKGROUND

The New York City poverty program is directed by the Council Against Poverty, which was established by executive order of the Mayor in 1966. The Council is composed of 51 members: 25 from the designated poverty areas of the city, 17 public officials, and nine from the private sector.

The Council is the policymaking body for the annual distribution of some $70 million of antipoverty funds.

OEO versatile funds account for approximately $16 million annually of the total funding. These OEO funds for the most part are channelled into 26 target areas based on a "Fair Share" allocation. "Fair Share" is determined by a formula involving the number of persons receiving welfare, juvenile delinquency rates, number of live births on general service and six other contributing factors.

Each of the 26 poverty areas so designated is represented by a Community Corporation, which administers the funds allocated to its area.

The elected board of directors of each Community Corporation approves program proposals for its area within its budget allocation which must then receive final approval from the Council Against Poverty.

BASIS OF SURVEY

Mr. Elly Rosen, representing the Association of Jewish Anti-Poverty Workers, testified June 25, 1971 before an ad hoc subcommittee on Education and Labor that "Jews in NYC, are systematically denied participation in anti-poverty programs."

Pursuant to this allegation, Congressman James Scheuer

requested Mr. Frank Carlucci, Director of OEO, to look into the validity of the complaint.

METHODOLOGY

All efforts to locate valid conventional statistical data on the current location, number, and income of Jews in New York City were fruitless. It was therefore conceived that the executive directors, board members, and other key staff personnel of the 26-area antipoverty corporations should be able to provide the most reliable ethnic estimates of their constituencies. Consequently, all 26 corporations were contacted and estimates obtained.

While the technique appears to have yielded reasonably consistent data, there were some exceptions. In the Lower East Side, for example, the staff people interviewed contend that there were less than 1,000 income-eligible Jews. More authoritative data from a Census Bureau study, and another from the Department of Labor, plus information from local settlement houses indicate that there are considerably more.

A similar situation exists in Morrisania and Brownsville, where the staff indicated there were no eligible Jews, yet local Jewish leaders and sociologists contend there is an appreciable number of impoverished elderly Jews living in the areas.

It must also be noted that personnel in four of the area corporations were unable to furnish an estimated ethnic or religious breakdown on the number of participants in the poverty programs in their area. Some of these officials excused their inability to provide this information on the basis of the fact that delegate agency reports go directly to the CDA, which is the administrative staff of the Council Against Poverty.

FINDINGS

Mr. Rosen's allegation that Jews are systematically excluded from participation in New York's poverty program, while imprecise, is not totally devoid of validity. The two poverty areas, (Williamsburg and Crown Heights) with an appreciable number of Jewish poor have good Jewish participation as recipients, staff and board members. This survey strongly indicates two things. First, where and insofar as Jews are excluded from poverty program participation, it is less because they are Jewish than because they are elderly. Second, their group characteristics do not relate to the indices originally used by the Poverty Council to determine target areas. Prime examples of this situation are Far Rockaway and Coney Island. Ninety thousand of the 97,000 total population of Far Rockaway are estimated to be Jewish. It is further estimated that approximately 18,000 of these are impoverished elderly Jews. The Far Rockaway poverty program, however, limits its services to five small target areas consisting of 5,000 poor, of whom 90 percent are black, 8 percent are Puerto Rican and 2 percent are "white" and predominantly Jewish.

A similar situation exists in Coney Island, where the poverty program target area encompasses 40,000 poor, 70 percent of whom are black or Puerto Rican. Yet most of the remaining 70,000 people on Coney Island are low-income, elderly Jews, many of them living in public housing projects. It is reported that they participate in large numbers in senior citizen organization activities, although these are not funded by OEO antipoverty funds.

In three other poverty areas (Lower East Side, Brownsville, and Morrisania), the area corporation staff members interviewed contend there are few if any impoverished Jews. But Jewish leaders, as well as other authoritive sources, insist these areas contain significant numbers of elderly Jewish poor. The fact that these folk seem invisible to their area poverty program staff gives credence to Rosen's allegation that Jews are under-served.

Unlike most other area corporations which have been operational to some degree for four years, the Bronx River Corporation is only now becoming incorporated. The lag is reflected in the fact that the BRC has but one active program, Neighborhood Youth Corps, in which participation is estimated at 55 percent black, 40 percent Puerto Rican, 4 percent other, and 1 percent Jewish. By comparison, Jewish low-income folks are estimated to constitute about 3 percent of the target area population. This discrepancy appears to corroborate the comments that a high proportion of the low-income Jews are elderly, and that for the elderly all too little provision is made. The fledgling BRC is now conducting neighborhood surveys to identify needs, and Jewish and other elderly participation may rise as appropriate programs are initiated.

By contrast in nearby Tremont, with 7,000 improverished Jews out of a total target area population of 118,853, the area corporation runs a senior citizens' program in which elderly Jewish participation is estimated at almost one fifth of the total.

The other area corporations have essentially no low-income Jewish residents.

While OEO allocates only $492,000 annually for senior citizens' programs in New York City (out of its $8,000,000 national budget), the City's elderly are not entirely without assistance. The City of New York operates 26 senior citizens' centers, and these are augmented by like operations funded through private organizations.

Table 1 shows the funding and the population and participation breakdowns of the 25 area poverty corporations.

Table 1. Estimated Poverty Program Participation in New York City (August 1971)

Corporation	Funding (thousands)	Population (thousands)			Staff			Percentage Participation				Board Members Jewish
		Total	Poverty	Jewish Poverty	Jewish	Other	Total	Spanish Speaking	Black	Jewish	Other	
Fort Greene	$1,100.0	102	85	0.0	0	180	180	40	55	0.0	5.0	0
Bronx River	137.0	160	128	5.0	0	22	22	40	55	1.0	4.0	0
Tremont	697.2	119	101	7.0	0	57	57	46	37	a	17.0	7
Hunts Point	1,500.0	172	154	0.0	4	198	202	76	24	0.0	0.1	0
Morrisania	1,180.0	170	136	0.0b	4	83	87	33	66	0.0	1.0	0
South Bronx	447.2	110	61	0.5	5	51	56	50	40	1.0	9.0	1
East Harlem	462.0	145	101	0.0b	2	93	95	50	40	0.0	10.0	0
Lower East Side	1,700.0	200	180	1.0c	15	85	100	a	a	a	a	2
Lower West Side	729.0	169	54	6.4	3	22	25	53	17	7.0	23.0	6
Mid-West Side	482.0	208	51	0.0	1	37	37	a	a	a	a	13
Upper West Side	480.0	209	135	2.0	1	111	112	48	38	0.5	14.0	6
Central Harlem	3,600.0	287	160c	0.0	0	800	800	5	95	0.0	0.0	0
Coney Island	476.1	110	40d	6.0d	3	20	23	55	45	0.0	0.0	3
South Brooklyn	1,180.9	221	148	0.0	0	207	207	47	39	0.0	14.0	0
Sunset Park	219.0	75	52	0.0	0	11	11	80	6	0.0	14.0	0
Williamsburg	1,380.3	190	175	33.0	55	199	254	39	28	33.0	0.0	13
Bedford-Stuyvesant	2,100.0	476	450	0.2	6	804	810	20	80	0.0	0.0	2
Brownsville	979.5	130	100	0.0d	7	69	76	34	66	0.0	0.0	1
Bushwick	750.4	200	75	0.0d	1	25	26	30	40	0.0	30.0	0
Crown Heights	695.0	250	215	56.2	7	17	24	a	a	a	a	18
East New York	1,218.0	100	70	0.7	0	22	22	50	50	0.0	0.0	1
Rockaway	200.0	97e / 5a	25e / 5a	18.0c / 0.1a	1	20	21	20	75	0.0	5.0	5
Corona-E. Elmhurst	272.8	80	36	0.0	0	21	21	25	75	0.0	0.0	0
Long Island City	547.7	78	59	0.0d	2	15	17	30	70	0.0	0.0	2
South Jamaica	971.0	218	72	0.0	0	137	137	a	a	a	a	0
Staten Island	200.0	90	15	0.15	0	14	14	20	70	1.0	9.0	2
Totals												
Number		4,274	2,858	138.14	116	3,320	3,436					5
Percent		100	66.6	3.1	(3.5)	(96.5)	(100)					

a. Sources claim no knowledge.
b. No known Jewish population, but Jewish staff members.
c. Target area only.
d. Inaccurate estimate; other sources indicate considerably more.
e. Total area population.

Re: Jewish Poverty
Sol Levy and Bernard Weinberger

The recent concern of the Jewish community, and
particularly the Federation, with poor Jews is commend-
able, but based on a distortion of the facts. Therefore,
we would like to submit some considerations for future
methods of dealing with the problem of the Jewish poor.
We are motivated to do so because this recent upsurge
of interest in the problem appears to stem from the publicity that followed the disclosures concerning Jewish
poverty that were made before the Congressional Committee meeting here in New York—and this publicity, we
feel, has left many people with a mistaken impression of
the current situation.

Let us begin by indicating that the poverty program
as presently constituted does not really cope with alleviat-
ing poverty; it does not deal with getting people out of
poverty in any meaningful way. Rather, the primary
thrust of the poverty program at this point is more an
effort to provide indigenous leadership for the poor;
to teach them to articulate their needs, make known
their demands, and to some extent, provide the mechanisms
for making their concerns known to the appropriate
levels of government.

By way of illustration, the poverty program is probably
the one vehicle that is most responsible for the effort to
decentralize the school system. At the same time, however,

evidence that the program does not really alleviate poverty
is provided by those poverty workers who take pride in the
fact that they have been able to add larger numbers
to the welfare rolls. Ever since the start of the poverty
program in New York City, which recruits local personnel to motivate poor people to demand their rights,
there has been a groundswell of new welfare recipients.
Undoubtedly, the poverty program has had many ben-
eficial and salutary effects. It has, in fact, been extremely
successful in developing leadership on a local level within
the black and Puerto Rican communities. We must
try to recognize the poverty program for what it is. At
its worst, it is simply a new form of political patronage
to the poor. At best, it is helping poor people to become
more politically sophisticated and more articulate in
spelling out their needs and their wishes; even so, this
has little to do with actually helping poor families.

Most of New York City's poverty funds are currently
being spent for the various programs' central administrative staffs. By way of illustration, Williamsburg has an
annual allocation of $1,300,000 of which $700,000 is spent
on central administrative costs, primarily personnel.
When you add to that the personnel costs of the so-
called delegate agencies, you come up with a figure of
close to $1,000,000—which means that only a small
fraction of the total area allocation is really spent on program content. Again we emphasize that we are not trying
to cast doubt on the inherent merit of our poverty programs. After all, such expenditures are necessary—since
personnel is a key element in motivating people. But all
the talk that these staff persons are helping poor people
pull themselves up by their own bootstraps is nothing
but a myth.

Even if Jews had meaningful representation on the
local boards, they would not deal realistically with Jewish
poverty. We have to clearly understand that the politics

of poverty have nothing to do with the substantive problems of poverty. Of course, Jews have every right to demand representation and a fair share of the action in all aspects of the poverty program. But what is significant is the fact that the corporations as presently constituted provide no means for removing people from poverty. Moreover, the thrust of community action is simply not what the Jewish community needs. The Jewish community is in a totally different state of development from other ethnic communities in New York City and has to be looked upon from a completely different perspective. We do not need community action. We are blessed with many organizations that can motivate and help Jewish people. The Jewish poor can only be helped in significant ways if poverty funds are directed towards actual training programs, and towards the actual alleviation of poverty. This has absolutely nothing to do with the 26 existing Community Corporations.

Moreover, we must remember that, while the argument of negligence applies to poor Jews, it can also be applied to many other minority groups throughout the city. Similarly, the argument that the concept of geographical boundries tends to limit the aid available to those poor people who live outside the boundaries cannot be confined to the Jews. For example, at the northern tip of Williamsburg, there is a good deal of poverty among the Polish, who are totally neglected by the official programs.So this is not a Jewish problem per se; it is a problem that can include all poor people.

One further point should be made: poverty, as we Jews speak of it, is not necessarily the same thing as "poverty" as defined by the government. The federal guidelines, of an annual income of $3800 for a family of two and $500 for each subsequent dependent, is a totally unrealistic figure for residents of urban centers. It is an even more unrealistic figure for Jews. When we speak of poverty, we are not necessarily limited to that narrow conception of the term. We are also talking of the family of four that makes $5000 or $6000 per year but that has to use its income to pay for Yeshiva tuition, for religious expenses, for special food needs and for an entirely different lifestyle than that of non-Jewish poor people. The government's guidelines ignore these expenses, which are necessary for a Jewish family. Thus, by the narrow definition of the government, many severely deprived Jewish people would not be considered poor.

The figures on Jewish poverty that have been quoted recently are exaggerated. The kind of poverty defined by government is not prevalent in Crown Heights, and not even in Williamsburg. But take, for example, our Jewish aged. A widowed Jewish woman lives alone on a mere subsistance level, but because she has $3000 in the bank— which she regards as more precious than her right hand—is not eligible for government assistance. Because she still has a savings, she is not entitled to supplemental welfare assistance. Yet, realistically speaking, she is a poor Jewish woman in need of governmental assistance. At present, however, our government's concept of poverty is totally different from ours. Its poverty guidelines are so construed as to identify only blacks and Puerto Ricans as the target population.

The most important aspect of dealing with Jewish poverty is in the area of training, since even those Jews who are employed tend to be underemployed. This is largely due to the fact that most Jews, particularly those who arrived in the United States after World War II, were poorly trained and therefore ill-equipped to compete in today's technologically-oriented society. Their only skills are the industriousness and aggressiveness of the Jewish entrepreneur. In fact, today even those Jews who live beyond the poverty line are doing so only because they are putting in 60 and 70 hours of work a week, instead of the customary 40.

It is not uncommon to find Orthodox Jews working a full day Sunday and putting in late hours at the knitting factory, making ties, or working in diamonds. This fellow, who is eking out $200 a week for his family of 8, 10, 12, or even 14, is doing so by risking his health and at the cost of the time he might be spending with his wife and children.

The primary problem, therefore, even for those people who are living "decently," is the question of under-employment and unemployment. This problem must be dealt with through meaningful training programs. There are currently city, federal and state-funded programs that deal with training; but all of them are either located in faraway ghetto areas, or else they are so predominantly non-Jewish that few of the Jewish people feel welcome in these programs. Few Orthodox Jews, Hasidic Jews, or any of the Jewish poor are enrolled in any existing training programs. The Port Authority Program, reputed to be an excellent one, likewise has few Jews enrolled, as do the Bedford Stuyvesant, or the Bay Ridge Manpower Center programs. The point is that there are no programs specifically geared to serve Jews.

Through a politically motivated effort on the part of an aspirant for public office, we in Williamsburg were able to negotiate a program in conjunction with the Pratt Institute, located in the immediate environs of Williamsburg, to train Hasidic and Orthodox boys in computer training. The YM & YWHA of Williamsburg was the source of recruitment for these trainees. One of the most gratifying aspects of any of our efforts has been the fact that, in that one year of training (during which all of the enrollees received stipends under the Manpower Training Development Act—funded with federal monies, through the State of New York), each one of the enrollees was ultimately placed in a position in the computer processing field which today earns him an annual salary of more than $10,000. This is a clear illustration of a meaningful way in which 30 Jewish families were assured that, under normal circumstances, they would never again be poor.

Obviously the computer field is a difficult one in which to achieve a high standing without a college degree, but these boys have all done well. This costly program has paid off. If one were to multiply this kind of program a hundred-fold, or a thousandfold, it would make the poverty program meaningful. Similiar programs for training poor Jews should be explored in areas other than the computer field.

Training would also be a meaningful program for senior citizens. During the period of registration for Medicare, poor senior citizens were employed to help register others. This provided senior citizens with an unprecedented experience in meaningful work that gave them a sense of true dignity and importance. We feel that such a program of employing senior citizens to help others would be immensely valuable. For example, we have groups of senior citizens and elderly Hasidic families travelling three times a day to Kingsbrook Medical Center to feed the chronically ill. They are extremely enthusiastic about this, and it gives them a tremendous sense of achievement. Similar programs could be developed in all Federation hospitals, providing volunteers with a token payment for lunches, dinners and carfare.

The question of what fields in which to train the Jewish poor is a valid one, since not all professions are conducive to their lifestyle. In general frontline jobs where the employees are directly involved with the consumer, are not appropriate for Hadisic Jews. Yet they can be trained in a host of other areas. The data processing field is just one of these. We feel that a middle management type of administrative job in the Federation network of hospitals would be an excellent resource for training young Hasidic Jews. Training in the electrical and mechanical fields, business management, and preparation for civil service work in

such fields as housing, health, and new fields such as
consumer affairs and environmental protection, provided
that it could be neighborhood-based, would also be useful.
The important thing about any training program, is that
we have to be sure that at the end of the line, there will
be jobs available to the trainees that will provide salaries
of at least $100 a week for single people and $150 a week for
people with families.

Education. It is clear that most of the young Jewish poor
are handicapped because of their lack of education.
No one in the Jewish community has yet provided a
tailor-made program for Jews that would enable them to
earn a high school equivalency, but this could easily be
done. One woman was able to develop a Woman's Talent
Corps almost singlehandedly; it now provides a state-
recognized equivalent of the Associate Arts degree,
that helps paraprofessionals get jobs requiring college
degrees. Her program is now run with government funds,
even though she started out with very little money. Many
of the community colleges have extension programs
that use only government funds, none of which filters down
to the Jewish community; this situation could also be
changed.

Legal services. The federal government is currently
providing funds through the city and the Council Against
Poverty for Community Action Legal Services—CALS—to
the tune of $4,300,000 annually. This provides neighbor-
hood-based, free legal services for the poor. Our experience
has been that most of these centers—the one in Williamsburg, for example—clearly exclude Jews from their
services. The Federation recently gave COLPA (the
National Jewish Commission on Law and Public Affairs)
$10,000. However, its services relate only to general
public issues; thus the average poor Jew must still pay a
lawyer's fee in a landlord-tenant case, divorce proceeding or
in criminal court. Unless there is a public official—such as

an Assemblyman or Councilman—who is occasionally willing to provide help without charge, there are no free legal services available for poor Jews. It should be a relatively simple matter for the Lawyers' Division of the Federation to set up such a program in several key Jewish neighborhoods.

Health center. Through the city, the federal government spends $4 million each year for health centers in poverty areas. But not one penny of this money touches the Jewish community. There is no reason why Williamsburg-Crown Heights, or for that matter Rockaway, cannot have something similar to the Provident Medical Society now located in Bedford-Stuyvesant.

Housing. Housing is probably the most significant aspect of all poverty; yet it is a subtle problem, and one which is often not associated with Jewish poverty. Thousands of poor Jews are imprisoned in homes, both public and private, that they moved into when the neighborhood was still a thriving Jewish community. They are now too poor to move out with the others. While the Federation has no particular role in the housing field, it is clear that any strategy that deals with poverty should incorporate a concern with housing. We anticipate that the most explosive issue in the Jewish community during the next year or two will be the placing of low-income housing in areas densely populated by Jews, such as the Forest Hills project on 108th Street and the Lindenwood project near Howard Beach.

Loan fund. Since it is generally recognized that Jewish poverty is usually associated with the Orthodox segment of the community, the simplest way for the Federation to have an impact on the Jewish poor would be through the Yeshivas, which have the largest constituency of Orthodoxy. Even if the Federation finds it impossible to provide direct grants for Yeshivas, through its resources the Federation could still provide loans to Yeshivas for construction or operating budgets. The interest rates paid by Yeshivas for their constant and recurrent loans are staggering. Through a consortium of banks and Federation "clout," these loans could be made available to the Yeshivas, thus aiding them considerably, without actually spending any money.

Traditional services. The traditional services provided by the Federation agencies such as JFS, JBG, JCCA, etc., which have emphasized a one-to-one relationship over the years, are no longer sufficient to deal with the size of the problems in the Jewish community. New techniques of dealing with group problems and avoiding the long waiting lists have to be developed to meet these challenges.

Community involvement. The traditional role of the community center has to be altered considerably. We can no longer wait for people to come to the center for service; rather, the center itself must begin to move out to reach the community. In the two areas of Williamsburg and Crown Heights where poverty funds are available, the Jewish community has developed their own community action organizations. In Williamsburg, the United Jewish Organizations, and in Crown Heights the Jewish Community Council of Crown Heights, serve as excellent means for reaching the local Jewish communities. In these areas, there is little for the Federation to do. But in those areas where no such funds are available, the community center should become deeply involved in all of these issues.

The Educational Alliance is only beginning to scratch the surface in terms of becoming involved with the Orthodox leadership and getting to the heart of the issues of the Jewish community. For example, the Alliance is not at all involved in the issue of the low-income project now planned for Norfolk Street, on the Lower East Side. The Bronx House sits right in the middle of one of the largest Jewish communities in the Bronx on Pelham

Parkway, but it has little to do with the community as a whole beyond servicing those who come to it. The Inwood "Y" is just a few blocks away from Rabbi Breuer's Adat Jeshurun, the largest German-Jewish community in the country. They are now being threatened by the installation of a combination school-housing complex, and the situation is made more awkward since the "Y" has little rapport with that community. The same is true of the Boro Park "Y," even though it has some programs to service the Orthodox community. The question here is of involvement that goes beyond immediate and direct services.

We also feel that community centers in non-poverty areas where there are no funds, should provide a staff person to work outside the community center and help organize the Jewish community, serving as its director. Most of the Jewish communities lack the basic funds necessary to organize themselves. The contribution of one staff person might mark the beginning of a remarkable rejuvenation of the community.

Legislative lobbying. A great many people feel that the best thing that could happen to the poverty programs would be for them to halt completely. At this late stage of the game, however, that is very unlikely to happen. The alternate solution is to lobby for the kind of effective legislation that would change the structure of the program. The recent involvement with the decentralization schemes proposed by Human Resources Administration Administrator Sugarman and the Comprehensive Health Planning Program are only indications of what is yet to come in other areas. The Federation has to become involved in all of this at the outset, so that this trend does not ignore the Jewish community.

A case in point is the recent legislation authorized by the House which would permit non-poverty families to use the facilities of day care centers and be charged fees in accordance with their ability to pay. If this kind of philosophy were extended to Headstart and other poverty programs, we could undo the current stranglehold of one or two ethnic groups on poverty funds.

1. To involve ourselves now in the Community Corporations would be a mistake. Even if sufficient funds were available, the ethnic hostilities engendered by such a move would simply not be worth the effort.
2. The Federation and its affiliate agencies should circumvent the New York City Council Against Poverty and apply for direct grants on specific programs to OEO, the Labor Department, HEW, the Office of Minority Enterprises of the Commerce Department, HUD and even the Agriculture Department. (A case in point: Mobilization for Youth never got a dime from New York City, and yet it has spent millions every year that it gets directly from Washington, specifically under OEO 207 demonstration grants.)
3. Watch carefully for the new legislation and new trends in government that are the key to the problems that the Jewish community will face in the future.

4. ON ENDING JEWISH POVERTY

The Jewish Hospital and the Jewish Community

William Kavesh

The vaunted ability of the American community to raise money has been satirized so much that it is not surprising to discover that very few people have any idea what Jewish fund-raising organizations (federations) do. The term "federation" has arisen to describe the umbrella organizations of the local Jewish communities. Historically, Federations resemble the traditional Jewish communities of Europe, in that they raise money for various communal needs. However, the voluntaristic, democratic American Jewish community differs substantially from the European *Kehillah* which was frequently sanctioned by the state and given civil, social and cultural responsibilities. The American Federation arose more as a convenient aggregation of independent agencies for the purposes of fund-raising than from a coherent community plan. Federations have evolved into communal organizations which, by virtue of their wealth (Federation campaigns raised over $ 250,000,000 in 1969), constitute a major element in urban Jewish communities. They fund local organizations as diverse as Jewish centers, Hebrew schools, hospitals, family services, vocational aid, and lately, Hillels and Jewish student projects. A substantial portion of Federation capital goes to Israel through the United Jewish Appeal and the Israel Emergency Fund. Federations even give support to organizations ordinarily thought of as independent national groups, such as the American Jewish Committee and the Anti-Defamation League.

The national organization of the Federations is the Council of Jewish Federations and Welfare Funds (CJFWF). It is this group whose annual meeting in Boston in 1969 was picketed by Jewish youth who felt that something was wrong with Federation priorities. Federation priorities currently include Jewish hospitals—which comprised 42.3 percent of Federation budgets in 1967.[1] Yet, despite the fact that Federations allotted more than 40 percent of their 1967 budgets to hospitals, these funds made up only 2.8 percent of the expenditures of Jewish hospitals in that year. The continuing substantial drain on Federation funds by hospitals, in an era of re-evaluation of the validity of community services in light of community needs, has prompted this inquiry.

When Mt. Sinai Hospital opened in 1852 in New York City, its Articles of Incorporation stated that "The particular business purpose and object of such association and society will be medical and surgical aid to persons of Jewish persuasion." Two days before it opened, the hospital board passed a resolution "that the Visiting Committee be instructed not to receive any patients other than Jews except in cases of accident."[2] This policy lasted until 1865, when Mt. Sinai's doors were opened freely to all members of the community. Since that time, the percentage of Jewish patients in Jewish-sponsored hospitals has steadily dropped, to 60 percent in 1933, and 35 percent in 1964.[3] In some areas, the change has been quite striking. Mt. Sinai Hospital in Chicago now resides in a black ghetto, where 11 percent of the in-patients and 7 percent of the out-patients are Jewish.[4] Even fewer Jews express a preference for Jewish hospitals—17 percent in one study.[5] On the other hand, the constituency of a

Jewish family service may exceed 90 percent Jewish.

It is not surprising, then, that the rationale for the so-called Jewish hospital has been under scrutiny for some time. One may obtain some perspective on the rather tortuous reasoning that has been advanced today to justify the Jewish hospital by briefly reviewing some history. Jews have been most reluctant to put it into print, but the early rationale for Jewish hospitals is all too obvious—religious discrimination. The 1958 anniversary celebration of one prominent Jewish hospital put it in this way:

> There was a feeling that people needed an institution sympathetic to their religious views, and where those who needed it could be served food that was prepared according to Jewish dietary laws. Furthermore, the population was rapidly increasing, and more of the Jewish faith were entering the field of medicine. It was difficult for able Jewish physicians to gain staff membership in other hospitals. . . .[6]

Would-be Jewish nurses had a similar predicament. Herman Dana, in *The Early Days of the Beth Israel*, notes that "The establishment of the Nurses' Training School in the summer of 1918 gave to Jewish girls for the first time an opportunity to become nurses under completely friendly auspices. Hitherto, they had complained of hostility and prejudice in non-Jewish institutions with the result that there were only 8 registered [Jewish] nurses in Boston at that time."[7]

This type of rationale persisted for a surprisingly long time.[8] However, in the past 20 years, discrimination against Jews in hospital facilities has ceased to be an issue. The kosher TV-dinner has become a fixture at Catholic and nonsectarian voluntary hospitals, to say nothing of the Jewish hospital where kosher kitchens have been rapidly disappearing. Likewise, Jewish religious services are held as regularly at nonsectarian hospitals as at the hospitals under Jewish auspices. As for the needs of the Jewish doctor, the proponents of the Jewish hospital have seen the handwriting on the wall for 10 years now. Not to be outflanked by anyone, they have responded by debunking the whole issue of the Jewish doctor. At the 1963 Council of Jewish Federations and Welfare Funds General Assembly, Cecil Sheps, then at the University of Pittsburgh but formerly executive director of Boston's Beth Israel Hospital, asserted:

> The first objective of philanthropic support by the organized Jewish community for hospital and medical care programs generally, should not be to meet the total needs of Jewish doctors in the conduct of their practices or to meet the needs of all the Jewish people for hospitalization and medical care. To do so would presuppose a type of ghettoization which is retrogressive, undesirable, and unnecessary.[9]

Now that what had been seen as the prime justification of Jewish hospitals is no longer relevant, some mighty specious logic has been invoked to rationalize the continuation of their funding by the Jewish community. The multiplicity of proposals is perhaps the best proof of the inability of the Jewish hospital proponents to construct convincing arguments. It has been suggested that "the special sectarian drive is endowed with the motivation to get things done," and that "as long as we are a religious nation. . . it would seem that sectarian hospitals should still continue to be available."[10] What should be noted, however, about America's historic sectarianism is that it stems directly from the Middle Ages, when the only people who went to hospitals were those who couldn't afford to have a physician care for them at home. At that time, charitable endeavors were traditionally the responsibility of the religious sects, and this pattern persisted through the early history of this country. The Kaiser-*Permanente* and similar health care systems are witness to the fact that the private sector can deal adequately with these formerly sectarian domains. Sectarian hospitals should be no more normative than Sunday Blue Laws.

Closely aligned with the "sectarian drive" argument is the contention that the Jewish community's image is at stake in the delivery of health services and that therefore Jewish community. . . should do its generous share,"[11] Variations on this theme abound: "Our Jewish hospitals are in the midst of all this; when they do something right it is a credit to the Jewish community and when they do something wrong, there can be adverse consequences not only for the hospital but for the entire Jewish group."[12] "The Jewish community owes the contribution it makes to rest of the community because it is a prestigious segment of the population,"[13] This type of defensive posture stems, no doubt, from legitimate insecurities which affect those who grew up in an age when anti-Semitism was rampant. However, it is alien to today's young people and does not reflect contemporary realities.

Recent data have compared Jewish attitudes ten years ago with those today on the question of what is a "good Jew." On the question "gain respect of Christian neighbors," ten years ago 59 percent of Jewish adults questioned thought it was "essential." In a study just completed, 23 percent of adults and 16 percent of youth feel it is essential.[14] In sum, then, the sad fact that discrimination against Jews forced them to set up their own hospitals does no honor to the Jewish community and imposes no responsibilities upon it. One might as well argue for continued discrimination against Jews, since *that* has plenty of historical precedent. The Catholic Church saves the community a lot of money by running parochial schools, but no Jew ever argued for day schools because we must do our "generous share."

The third historical argument stems from what might be categorized as Jewish cultural-religious-sentimental needs

—what are described as "intrinsic Jewish reasons" in a 1969 CJFWF paper by Lloyd Schwenger, president of the Cleveland Federation. "The hospital represents a major philanthropic interest for many members of the Jewish community. . . major area of involvement for the Jewish volunteer . . . provides a Jewish environment . . . special opportunity for the training of the Jewish physician."[15] It has been amply demonstrated above that the trappings of Jewish "environment"—kosher food, services, etc.—are readily available in nonsectarian and Catholic hospitals.[16] Furthermore, there are serious questions as to the degree to which Jewish hospitals do, in fact, satisfy legitimate Jewish needs. One of the most outspoken proponents of Jewish-sponsored hospitals, Dr. Morris Hinenburg, medical care consultant to the Federation of Jewish Philanthropies of New York, notes in an address that "those of of us who are here are not entirely unaware of the fact that many hospitals under Jewish auspices have only met in varying degree the requirements of observant Jews."[17] In New York City, an observant Jewish intern in internal medicine can arrange to be off duty on the Sabbath at Coney Island Hospital, a city-operated hospital, but not at Montefiore, a Federation hospital. Regarding Jewish doctors, it would seem that Dr. Sheps' pronouncements should be enough to dispose of the "special opportunity for the training of Jewish physicians" issue. Nonetheless, Jewish medical training continues to be a theme in the proponents' arguments—which range from references to the "historic role of Jewish scholars in the field of medicine" to dire hints at quotas and other possible restrictions "at some future date."[18] Early Jewish scholars also had traditional ties to hand-crafts and commerce, yet very few people have suggested that the Jewish community subsidize trade or business schools. If the time comes when restrictions occur on Jewish access to hospitals, one suspects that the general environment won't be too healthy for Jews anyway and that Jewish hospitals won't solve the problem. "The establishment of medical schools under Jewish sponsorhip" has even been touted as a justification for continuing Federation support for Jewish hospitals. Yet, it is of interest to note that when Albert Einstein College of Medicine became the first American Jewish-sponsored medical school in 1955, its primary affiliated teaching hospital was Abraham Jacobi Hospital—operated by the City of New York. Its later affiliation with Montefiore Hospital was due to a variety of factors—among the least of which was Montefiore's sponsorship by the New York Federation.

With respect to the "Jewish volunteer," she is in evidence at any hospital where there is a substantial Jewish constituency—including most suburban and community hospitals. It can also be argued that the Jewish community could benefit far more if all this manpower were to devote itself to more legitimately Jewish causes—the problems of Soviet Jewry and Jewish education, for example.

The final aspect of the historical argument is the notion that "the hospital represents a major philanthropic interest for many members of the Jewish community." It has been noted that "hospital boards as groups often represent the largest contributors to the Welfare Fund campaign, ranging as high as 30 percent of the annual amount raised."[19] With the inordinate prestige which wealth affords in this country, it is not difficult to see the obvious implications of the foregoing statement. This will be dealt with in more detail further on.

The second broad category of arguments for the retention of Jewish Hospital Federation affiliation is the "ought to" argument. Faced with the inexorable logic that the original criteria for the affiliation of the Jewish hospital with the Jewish Federation no longer have any basis, the proponents of Jewish hospitals have devised a number of suggestions as to new roles for Federation money; "developing a pattern of direct financial underpinning for specific services which are required by the community and for which other sources are not available";[20] "develop and put into practice important concepts in scientific medicine and medical care delivery";[21] "improvement of crisis care";[22] "new buildings... new apparatus... research."[23] In Montreal, where the government largely finances all hospitals, including Jewish ones "grants are made for ... research, chief of medicine, certain excluded services (TB) and bank interest on capital loans."[24]

All these suggestions contradict one fundamental premise which even Dr. Morris Hinenburg advocates: "Federation's function must now depend less on providing services and more on providing a means of identification and a perpetuation, strengthening of the Jewish community. Federation must be an instrument for the benefit of the total Jewish community and not alone for its constituent agencies."[25] When one asks what conceivable benefit accrues to the Jewish community from supporting the research of a chief of medicine or improving an emergency room which is less and less frequented by Jews, the answer is obvious: nothing. The Jewish community might as well give its money to Massachusetts General Hospital in Boston or Columbia-Presbyterian in New York, because both do quality research. In Baltimore, there is a program to detect carriers of Tay-Sachs disease, a lethal disorder confined almost entirely to Jews.[26] This is one of the few examples of research in this country which the Jewish community can justify supporting. It is being conducted by the John F. Kennedy Institute Tay-Sachs program of the John Hopkins University Hospital—*not* by Mt. Sinai, the Federation Hospital of Baltimore. As a group, Jews don't need to support demonstration projects, medical education or research any more than Episcopalians, Chinese-Americans, or blacks do. One has more justification in organizing skiers to do orthopedic surgery research because they break more legs than the average non-skiers do.

The final areas in which it has been suggested that the Federation play a role are those of coordination, planning, and community-oriented ventures. However, coordination is at present the exception rather than the rule. In 1969, CJFWF published an extensive study by Harry Lurie of the relationships between Jewish hospitals and Jewish Federations.[27] Twelve of the thirty Jewish hospitals cited in Lurie's report had agreements with the federation or with service agencies to serve patients referred by them. In Boston at least, the financial arrangments are on a strict payment for service basis.[28]

There is no reason why Jewish agencies could not contract for services from any hospital—just as non-Jewish agencies do. Regarding planning, it is noteworthy that, while 11 of 13 federations replying to Lurie's questionnaire thought that they should be concerned with the professional standards of the hospital, 21 of 27 hospitals said no. Likewise, while a majority of federations replying felt that federations should be concerned with hospital administration, 25 of 28 hospitals said no. In 17 of 24 cities, hospitals have representatives serving on the Federation Board of Trustees. Only 3 of 24 federations reported reciprocal representation on the hospital boards.[29] Thus, the relationships established so far seem to be rather onesided.

The final suggestion as to the Federation's role in Jewish hospitals comes under the aegis of "community orientation." The Health Services Committee Task Force of the CJFWF reported in November 1970 on the "definition of the community-oriented dimensions of the Jewish hospital."[30] They defined three "communities—the total community, the Jewish community, [and] the community in which the hospital is located." Regarding the total community, it is clear that the Jewish hospital differs little from any voluntary hospital in its role regarding government, regional planning and third-party groups. All are affected equally.

Regarding the Jewish community, it is clear that caring for the Jewish poor is no justification for continued Federation support of hospitals: "Studies in New York over the years reveal that the need for the support of Jewish indigent sick in hospitals is relatively minor and could hardly constitute a justification for the costly capital and maintenance financing of Jewish hospitals."[31] The Task Force report confined the role of the Federation with regard to the Jewish community primarily to planning and coordination, which we have dealt with above.

It is with regard to a role in the community in which Jewish hospitals are located that the Federations have the least justification and the most to lose. The Task Force recommended priority attention to crisis care, differential relationships to selected groups of patients and attention to group practice. Again it should be noted that these have no more priority in a Jewish hospital than in any other; the Jewish community can give its money to any hospital which proclaims these goals. They are not uniquely Jewish.

What should be of concern to the Federation before it plunges into local community care is the nature of the polemics now erupting around the issue of community control. The Albert Einstein College of Medicine became deeply embroiled in the controversy involving control over Lincoln Hospital—a hospital which lies in the center of an urban ghetto and is staffed by Einstein for the City of New York. B'nai B'rith somewhat hastily concluded that anti-Semitism was behind some of the demands of the black and Puerto Rican community. The fact remains that, however complex the issues involved, Jewish Federations should look very carefully before getting unnecessarily involved in such issues. In particular, they should look with a somewhat jaundiced eye at the proposals made by Mitchell Rabkin, director of Boston's Beth Israel Hospital, at the 1969 CJFWF Meeting. [32] In discussing suggested federation concerns, Dr. Rabkin gratuitously notes that "Another focus is that of 'community representation,' *whatever that means*" (italics mine). A few pages later, he suggests that the Federation has an additional role as a "thoughtful voice of the consumer." He buttresses this with an emotional appeal to Jewish sentimentality (and no factual support) that if the Jewish-sponsored hospital "is abandoned by the federation, its excellence—a matter of fierce pride amongst us all—will be forced to subside," "What I am emphasizing is that there are mounting pressures upon hospitals from agencies which now control the majority of the hospital's dollars, and these agencies have no interest in the ethnic nature of our operation. The old situation of doing what's good for the Jews and being rewarded by an institution which happens to do good for most anyone else under its roof—this has changed to one where the pressures are to do what is good for the community in general. He who pays the piper calls the tune." [33] This is not a forum for an extended discussion of "community control." Suffice it to say that many responsible leaders feel that a community's say in services which affect it is not only desirable, but probably inevitable. With changing populations, this will invariably affect Beth Israel Hospital in Boston as much as Lincoln Hospital in New York. It would seem that what Dr. Rabkin wants to do is balance off the Jewish Federation as the "thoughtful voice of the consumer" against the "community representation" about which he speaks so contemptuously. The history of confrontations in New York City during the past five years should be enough to dissuade any Jewish group from being used as a buffer between a hospital administrator and the dissident groups he wants to ignore.

Suppose, then, that one confronts the logic that no real benefits accrue to the Jewish community from continued hospital affiliations. If the Jewish community withdraws its support, won't Beth Israel, Mt. Sinai and the rest go broke? Most indications suggest not.

Compare, for example, the annual statements for the year 1967 of Mt. Sinai and Columbia-Presbyterian Hospitals in New York City. Mt. Sinai is affiliated with the Federation of Greater New York. Columbia-Presbyterian has no sectarian affiliations. Their total operating expenditures are remarkably similar—almost $50,000,000.[34] Yet while Mt. Sinai received over one million dollars from Federation sources, Columbia-Presbyterian also managed to raise over a million dollars on its own initiative. It is apparent that a voluntary hospital can mount a substantial fund-raising campaign without resorting to sectarian sources. And the Federation is by no means the only source for Jewish-sponsored hospitals. In 1967, Beth Israel Hospital raised $453,000 from investments, contributions and its women's division, and was given $460,000 by the Combined Jewish Philanthropies of Boston.[35] Further, the New England Sinai Hospital, which derives substantial amounts of income from private Jewish philanthropy, nonetheless seems to function quite adequately without Federation support. The inevitable conclusion is that Federation support is not essential to solvency and that if it were to be withdrawn, it is highly unlikely that hospitals like Beth Israel and Mt. Sinai would fold.

If all this is so self-evident, one may ask, why are Jewish Federations still financing hospitals? The answer, which affords little comfort to those who believe in logic, is power, the monetary power alluded to earlier. The American Jewish community has to its credit chosen to invest much of its energy in charitable institutions. In the past, this meant hospitals, for all the historical reasons we have noted. The current American Jewish leaders have grown up in an era in which overt anti-Semitism was a reality—in which Jewish doctors were not the only ones who could not readily get the training and jobs they may have wanted. Hitler existed for them, not merely as a theological issue (as the Holocaust may confront Jewish youth today), but as the embodiment of an irrational hostility to the Jew which leaves the kind of impact that logical arguments do not always dent. The UAHC (Union of American Hebrew Congregations) study quoted above is important, not merely because it shows the changing attitudes of young Jews, but also because it points up the surprising degree to which adult Jews are motivated by the need to garner good will in the general community. "The largely subconscious fear of isolation, ghettoization and dependence on a potentially hostile community keeps Jews together paying for community services they no longer use but may someday need."[36] The American Jewish response to the 1967 Arab-Israeli war reflects similar fears.

Jewish youth are not unsympathetic to these fears. Yet, it is precisely because we are free from the direct effects of the traumatic experiences of the past 50 years that we can suggest that our perspective has validity. Dr. Rabkin says that the most important role for the federation in the future is to "work with the Jewish sponsored hospital to achieve congruence with the public demand for effectiveness."[37] We feel that the most important role for the federation in the future is to sponsor programs that contribute to creative Jewish survival. This means looking back at the past four thousand years and seeing what religious-cultural elements have made Judaism unique, then pursuing paths that have a reasonable possibility of perpetuating that tradition. We feel that the stagnation of contemporary Jewish life is so profound that unless the Federation devotes its energies to solutions of internal Jewish problems, a serious crisis of Jewish identity—now prevalent on campuses—may overspread much of the

Jewish community. Many of the leaders of American Jewry forget that their devotion to Jewish institutions is the legacy of a European culture which left them with emotional ties and some Yiddish, but little else concrete. Young Jews, especially on the campuses, do not have these ties. Morris Hinenburg is again apt when he notes "Unless the organized Jewish community reconstitutes itself to pursue Jewish objectives and to help descendents of Jewish immigrants to function discreetly as Jews, Federation and its agencies will not attract the loyalty of the younger generation,"[38]

Unfortunately, the fear of offending big contributors who support hospitals is a major motivating force for federation leaders, and if the response of the Boston Federation is any indicator, the whole issue of hospital financing will be swept under the rug. It is interesting that Irving Rabb, a Boston philanthropist who is among the most outspoken proponents of Jewish hospitals, should suggest an eminently sensible approach to the problem: "I do believe that we reckon best with the future by examining the past—without being bound by it—and considering the views of those most concerned with charting directions for the future."[39] Yet, when an attempt was made[40] to bring up the contents of this report for discussion before a committee of the Combined Jewish Philanthropies of Boston, it was noted that the material would have to be reviewed first to see if it was appropriate. After a month and a half of review, it was then noted that the material could not be presented until a rebuttal was written by hospital proponents. During this time, the $450,000 budget of Beth Israel Hospital was presented and approved with less discussion of its content than was devoted to the $2000 allocation for a Vocational Aid Society. Three months after the original suggestion, the material has still not been brought up for discussion. It is very difficult to understand why dedicated and conscientious leaders of the Jewish community want to insulate themselves from new approaches to Jewish hospitals when they have been so receptive to new ideas in other areas. A major factor lurking just below the surface seems to be fear of decreased federation contributions by hospital supporters. Contributions made on the basis of good will are presumably made by people of good will—otherwise, why charitable contributions at all? Why not simply self-indulgence? People of good will ought to be able to talk to each other without being completely befuddled by their emotions. If the Jewish community is afraid to embark upon new approaches to hospitals because entrenched hospital interests threaten overtly or by insinuation to cut their contributions to the federation, then the Jewish community is spiritually in bad shape. Men who make such petty threats hardly deserve to have their contributions designated as charity. Furthermore, there is no evidence that people with such conflicting motives about charitable endeavors constitute anything but a very small minority.

This is not to imply that people of good will who identify with the Jewish community cannot disagree. But at least relevant facts ought to be available and discussion should not take place under a sword of Damocles. There is no reason why in 50 years a contribution to Jewish education— to perpetuate Jewish culture—might not confer the same prestige as a contribution to a Jewish hospital does today. It depends entirely on where the organized Jewish community wants to place its stamp of approval. About the only thing these days that distinguishes man from a sophisticated computer is his ability to respond in a novel manner to completely new inputs. If we reject novelty, then we also reject, in large measure, our humanity.

The time has come for federation leaders to do some hard introspection; to confront past fears; to see if the needs of the Jewish community must still be met by a preoccupation with the "public demand for effectiveness." The abundant talents and energy of the Jewish Federation must be redirected toward areas which contribute to the enrichment of the quality of Jewish life—Jewish education, music, art, religious and secular culture. If there is anything to be learned from the black power movement, it is that each ethnic group has the right—and the obligation—to achieve its own self-advancement and self-fulfillment. Unless prestige in the Jewish community becomes associated with internal accomplishments, there will be very little to attract youth to Judaism. Social service is not sufficient justification for Jewish identity. The fitting epitaph to the age of American Jewry may well be that we died in our own hospitals.

NOTES

1. Harry Lurie, *Jewish Hospitals and Jewish Federations, A Study in Relationships* (New York: Council of Jewish Federations and Welfare Funds, 1969), p. 3.

2. Joseph Beka Hirsh and Doherty, *The Mt. Sinai Hospital in New York* (New York: Random House, 1952), pp. 15, 37.

3. Lurie, *Jewish Hospitals*, p. 35. Certain chronic care facilities, such as Beth Abraham in New York City, have maintained a higher percentage of Jews.

4. Data of the research department of the Jewish Federation of Metropolitan Chicago.

5. Morris Axelrod, et. al., *A Community Survey for Long Range Planning, A Study of the Jewish Population of Greater Boston,* (Boston: Combined Jewish Philanthropies of Greater Boston, 1967), p. 106.

6. *1958 Anniversary Celebration Program*, Beth Israel Hospital, Boston.

7. Herman Dana, *The Early Days of the B.I.,* 1911–20, (Boston: Printed Privately by Herman Dana, 1950).

8. *Planning for Federation Programs,* Proceedings, Jewish Federations of New York, Chicago, and Philadelphia, 1948, and "Bienenstock

Study," New York State Department of Education, Albany, 1950; "Wilson Report," New York State Board of Regents, Albany, 1953. As quoted in N.C. Belth, ed., *Barriers* (New York: Friendly House, 1958), p. 75.

9. *Major Issues Facing the Jewish Community—A symposium,* in Assembly Papers, CJFWF, New York, 1963.

10. Morris Hinenburg, *The Future of Jewish Philanthropy in the Health Field,* paper presented at the Second Western Conference for Executives of Selected Hospitals and Medical Centers, New Orleans, La., 1967.

11. Lloyd Schwenger, in *Federation-Hospital Planning and Financing Relationships,* Assembly Papers, CJFWF, New York, 1969, p. 17.

12. Ibid., p. 18.

13. Hinenburg, *The Future,* p. 13.

14. Leonard Fein and Bernard Reisman, Unpublished Data, Long Range Planning Project, Union of American Hebrew Congregations.

15. Schwenger, *Federation-Hospital,* p. 18.

16. In Boston, for example, St. Elizabeth's Hospital (Catholic), Peter Bent Brigham (nonsectarian), and Massachusetts General (nonsectarian) all have available a Jewish chaplain and kosher food for those who desire them.

17. Hinenburg, *The Future,* p. 9.

18. Benjamin Rosenberg, *Financing Jewish Hospitals, The Changing Role of Federations,* Assembly Papers, CJFWF, 1965, p. 6. Also Hinenburg, *The Future,* p. 16.

19. Rosenberg, *Jewish Hospitals,* p. 6.

20. Ibid., p. 6.

21. Mitchell Rabkin, In Assembly Papers, CJFWF, 1969, p. 1.

22. Irving Rabb, *Community Dimensions of the Jewish Hospital,* Report of the Health Services Committee Task Force, Assembly Papers, CJFWF, 1970, p. 4.

23. Hinenburg, *The Future,* p. 16.

24. Rosenberg, *The Future,* p. 9.

25. Hinenburg, *Jewish Hospitals and Jewish Federations,* p. 4.

26. See Joseph Polakoff, "Study Disease that Hits Jewish Children," in the *Boston Jewish Advocate,* May 20, 1971.

27. Lurie, *Community Dimensions,* p. 10.

28. Personal communication, Simon Krakow, Director, Jewish Family and Children's Service, Boston.

29. Lurie, *Jewish Hospitals and Jewish Federations,* pp. 8, 13.

30. Rabb, *The Future*, p. 1.

31. Hinenburg, p. 11.

32. Rabkin, Assembly Papers pp. 1–8.

33. Ibid., p. 6.

34. Annual Report, 1967, Mt. Sinai Hospital of New York. Annual Report, 1967, Columbia-Presbyterian Hospital, New York. Operating income for Mt. Sinai included contributions of $1,186,407 (apparently all from Federation sources, since no other breakdown is given), $186,850 from the Greater New York Fund, United Hospital Fund, and $414,037 in investment income, for a total of about $1,800,000. Columbia-Presbyterian had contributions and investment income totalling $1,172,598 (broken down, apparently, to $600,000 in contributions with the rest in investment; it is not clear where, if at all, the Greater New York Fund and United Hospital Fund fit in, since no breakdown is given). In 1967, Mt. Sinai had a $205,522 operating deficit; Columbia-Presbyterian had a net operating income of $1,438,117.

35. Annual report, 1966–67, Beth Israel Hospital, Boston. Beth Israel's budget was $12,000,000. Around the corner from B.I., the Peter Bent Brigham Hospital, a voluntary nonsectarian-sponsored hospital in the same year operated a budget of $16,000,000 with only $252,000 in investment income and gifts. They had a surplus of $16,000, whereas Beth Israel had a loss of $221,000. Annual report, 1967, Peter Bent Brigham Hospital, Boston.

36. Personal communication, Bernard Kutner, Director, Center for Social Research in Rehabilitation Medicine, Albert Einstein College of Medicine.

37. Rabkin, Assembly Papers, p. 6.

38. Hinenburg, *Jewish Hospitals and Jewish Federations*, p. 3.

39. Lurie, *The Future*, introduction.

40. By the author.

A Systematic Approach to Poverty Policy

Bruno Stein

Like the diet prescribed by doctors, which neither restores the patient nor allows him to succumb, so these doles that you are now distributing neither suffice to ensure your safety nor allow you to renounce them and try something else.

—Demosthenes

We return in this essay to the question of means and ends. What do we want to accomplish with respect to poverty? What methods are consistent with this goal? What role do income transfers play in this process? First, however, we must see to what extent poverty is a social problem. It is obviously a problem for the poor, most of whom do not enjoy their status. The poor, however, have little political power, since economic growth has succeeded in making them a minority, even when poverty is measured in relative terms. It is the non-poor who have the power. Therefore, programs dealing with poverty must come from them. The question is, do the non-poor see poverty as a problem? Political preoccupation with poverty, even after the official war on poverty ended, indicates that they do. There are a number of reasons for this concern on the part of the non-poor. They probably fear social disorder, either in terms of large-scale rioting or through antisocial behavior such as crime. Also, poverty in its more visible form is unesthetic. In addition, Judeo-Christian feelings of compassion and egalitarian ideas from their democratic heritage may play a significant role.

Still, the public may also feel that the present degree of poverty or economic inequality is necessary or desirable. One commonly cited reason is the need to maintain work incentives. The non-poor may believe, for example, that programs to shore up the poor encourage laziness. This reasoning is faulty, however, if, as our poverty profiles show, most of the poor cannot alter their status. To them, incentives are meaningless. I suggest that the threat of poverty is really an incentive to the non-poor, to work and save in order to maintain their status.

Poverty may also be necessary for the psychological well-being of the non-poor. To be well off means to be better off than somebody else. The non-poor may need the poor for comparison. It takes surprisingly little to place one in the highest ten percent of income receivers. In 1967, a taxable income of $14,000 did this; while $18,000 placed a tax unit in the highest five percent of taxpayers.[1] It is doubtful whether such income receivers think of themselves as rich, or even suspect how high they stand in the ranking of taxpayers. They do not think that they have "made it." Those families who are really in the middle (say $6,000 to $8,000 taxable income) probably feel that they are struggling hard. The poor are *their* point of reference.

If this is the case, then "eliminating poverty" by some absolute standard threatens the status of the non-poor, except for the really rich. Programs that promise to break the poverty cycle may also represent a threat, although a longer range one, since the promotion of upward mobility for some people also implies the promotion of downward mobility of others. Families in the middle class are anxious to preserve their status. One indication of this can be found in rates of college attendance. Over a forty-year period, the proportion of sons from low-status homes who finish college has changed only imperceptibly, while the proportion of sons of college alumni has doubled. [2]

There is less downward mobility in the United States than in countries like Britain, Canada, or Denmark. [3] This is not true for blacks, however. As a group, they are not able to pass family advantages on to their children. Even if a black man's father was a professional manager or proprietor, he will usually be an operative, service worker or laborer. By contrast, the majority of white men with higher white-collar backgrounds remain at their father's employment level. [4]

Thus, the general populace have two contradictory feelings regarding poverty: a desire to reduce poverty, and a need for its continued existence. If the non-poor make the rules, they will optimize between the disparate goals so that antipoverty efforts will only continue until the needs of the non-poor rather than those of the poor [5] are satisfied. This point can be altered by changing the political values of the non-poor—for example, by persuading the non-poor that it will benefit them to help the poor. Coalitions between the poor and elements of the non-poor can also be useful, but only if the poor have some power.

I shall not pursue the question of what the political prerequisites are for a vigorous antipoverty program. Although of crucial importance, they are beyond the scope of this work. Instead, I shall assume, perhaps optimistically, that the body politic is sufficiently bothered by poverty to be willing to do something about it. Effective action requires that the goals of a polity be consistent with the means employed.

Three possible goals for these antipoverty programs are analyzed below. For each I shall explore the limitations and the conditions that are necessary in order to effect that goal. Two of the goals are short-term—a reduction in relief dependency, and the reduction of poverty in the present generation. The third goal is long-term—the reduction of intergenerational poverty. Other goals are possible, of course, but the above three more or less reflect the political discussions of the past decade. Discussion of means will be confined to those that are within the value system of a reasonably democratic capitalist society—thus for example, we shall exclude from consideration the liquidation of the poor, as clearly violating this value system.

REDUCTION OF RELIEF DEPENDENCY IN THE SHORT RUN

To reach the first goal, a reduction in relief dependency of the present generation, there are two opposite approaches possible. One is to make relief hard to obtain, thus forcing members of the relief population to find alternative means of support. A second is to increase the productivity of the poor, to enable them to earn more than a poverty income. We shall emphasize the second of these approaches, but the first also requires a brief comment.

Restricting Access to Relief. The size of the relief population can be controlled by restricting access to relief. This is the classic Poor Law approach, and is still operative. Relief is not an open-ended system, since it is not a guaranteed minimum income. A necessary condition is the ability to vary the effective test of eligibility. This condition can be satisfied by making eligibility a matter for administrative discretion. This is, in fact, the common practice; relief is obviously easier to obtain in some states and localities than in others, even for people within the same categories. A second condition is the ability to vary the onerousness of relief. This power is held by relief administrators who possess a variety of weapons to harass recipients and applicants.[6] In the Family Assistance program (FAP) the work or training requirement can be interpreted broadly or narrowly and thus can be used as a method for controlling the number of recipients.

This approach obviously does nothing to reduce poverty. To be successful, it requires considerable power, and the power must be exercised in a cold-blooded and inhumane fashion. Historically, it has not worked well. The reader may recall that the English Poor Law Reform of 1834 envisioned the abolition of outdoor relief, yet outdoor relief continued to rise. Perhaps the public does not have a strong enough stomach for the thoroughgoing application of this approach (I hasten to add that I certainly do not advocate it). The compromise—some control over numbers, but not enough to keep the relief rolls from rising—leaves everyone dissatisfied.

Providing Human Capital. The second approach to our first goal involves providing human capital, through training programs and necessary support service such as minimal health care and child care. The constraint upon this is that it only applies to a particular segment of the poverty population. It does not apply to those who are handicapped by age, disability, lack of education, or other irreversible personal characteristics.[7] Nor does it apply to Aid for Dependent Children (AFDC) mothers who, due to their particular circumstances, would require incentives powerful enough to overcome the economic and other costs of leaving their children in the care of others. The stronger the incentive, the greater the cost.

It is pointless to endow people with human capital unless there will be jobs at the end of the process. Hence, two conditions are necessary. One is a situation of full employment, so that, in the aggregate, jobs are likely to be available. The second is that labor markets must operate well enough to bring vacant jobs and potential workers together. Racial barriers are an important labor-market imperfection. Their removal is vital if minorities are to benefit from the suggested policy.

These conditions can also be viewed as means toward an end. They conflict with other widely held goals—for example, the tight labor markets of a full employment policy create inflationary pressures. If full employment and price stability are not compatible, the society must determine which goal will dominate, or at least what an acceptable tradeoff will be. To the extent that price stability is preferred, employment opportunities (and output) are curtailed. Unemployment falls with particular severity on those who are at the margin of the labor market—that is, the poor.[8]

At first glance, improving the performance of labor markets seems an innocuous goal, except to particular workers or employers whose market power would be reduced. A "perfect" labor market, however, treats all workers with equivalent abilities as interchangeable. Racial and ethnic discrimination is therefore an imperfection of major proportions. To the extent that bigotry and racism are important values to majority group members, a conflict in goals exists. Of course, discrimination in the labor market is only one aspect of racial discrimination. By the time that blacks and other minorities enter the labor market, they already carry with them the effects of prior discrimination (such as poor education and environment) that may lower their productivity and thus "justify" exclusion or lower wages.

The difference in labor-market opportunities favors some whites. But the economy as a whole incurs losses, since output would be greater if the labor of blacks and other minorities were more efficiently utilized. This economic loss is too diffuse to be noticed—although it is quite substantial—and may possibly be overcome by the satisfaction that whites derive from their more favorable labor market opportunities.[9]

To reiterate, a policy of lessening dependency by the use of training programs is subject to the constraints—in that its applicability is limited to potential employables, a group that excludes important segments of the poverty population. Given this constraint, the conditions of full employment and a perfect labor market are necessary, although not sufficient. These conditions themselves redistribute income. Some people gain and others lose by inflationary pressures and by the removal of barriers in the labor market—but, since total output should rise, it may be possible to compensate the losers.

This may sound like an exercise in abstract welfare economic theory. Practical applications are possible, however. Fixed-income receivers lose by inflation, and transfer mechanisms can be devised to make up their losses. For example, Social Security or pension benefits could be adjusted to meet rising living costs. Workers who lose the protection of segregated labor markets—for example, when white and black seniority lines in a plant are merged— could receive a lump sum bonus. The wherewithal for the compensation would be the higher incomes emerging from the fuller utilization of resources. Part of this increased income would be captured by taxes and could then be redistributed.

Economic Incentives. Public assistance *with incentives* (or negative income tax plans) is often advocated as a way to decrease relief dependency. Again, we must remember that incentives are relevant only to the employable. For this target population, programs like FAP increase the number of people who receive transfers. A principal purpose of FAP is to introduce equity between the working and the nonworking poor. If the incentives work, some of the nonworking poor will be drawn into the labor market, and if they were previously totally dependent, their relative dependency decreases.[10]

If the public expect FAP to reduce the total number of people on the relief rolls, they will be disappointed. This is not a goal of the program; in fact this goal would conflict with FAP's goal of equity between the working and nonworking poor. The public's disappointment in this case may lead to pressures to utilize traditional Poor Law methods to restrict access to the income-transfer system.

The training and work requirements of FAP can be used for deterrence if the work offered is sufficiently disagreeable so that it becomes the equivalent of the workhouse test (a situation in which conditions are so bad that only those persons lacking any alternatives will accept living in it.)

The conditions of full employment and healthy labor markets, together with the offer of well-conceived training programs, will bring forth most labor-market eligibles. Compulsion can be set at minimal levels, sufficient to dig out a few of the "lazy poor," satisfy the general public's work ethic, and meet the political needs of legislators. If the two necessary conditions are *not* met, then compulsion becomes a costly and a futile matter.

Subsidized Jobs and Guaranteed Jobs. Two other means are often mentioned in working toward the goal of reduced relief dependency. One is subsidizing jobs in the private sector; the second is guaranteeing jobs in the public sector (government as employer of last resort). Both are partial means, since by themselves they do not go far toward achieving the goal. However, they are consistent with the goal, means, constraints, and conditions given above. Both can be used to supplement and sometimes complement training programs. Needless to say, any guarantee of employment raises the economic value of training programs in a benefit-cost calculation. Whether the higher value is real or spurious depends on whether the jobs are disguised transfer payments or whether they add to the output of the economy.

Subsidized jobs are generally on-the-job training programs in which the government absorbs the employer's cost of training. At the end of the training period the subsidy stops. The employer keeps those trainees whom he wants and needs, and attempts are made to place the rest. Since the training is highly specific, the ideal employer is the one who does the training.

Programs of this type can be quite valuable in tight labor markets; employers are likely to give good training, since they will want to keep some of the alumni. Labor-market operations can be improved as those who seek work but are not yet fully qualified are brought into contact with employers in need of labor. A good on-the-job training program can substantially increase the productivity of persons who were previously at the edge of the working world.

A major disadvantage is that subsidizing jobs offers an incentive to employers to hire the subsidized workers in preference to others, and to let them go when the subsidy stops. This is especially true when the skill requirements are not really high, so that the subsidized workers are merely cheap substitutes for available unsubsidized labor. There is more here than an abstract question of equity. The introduction of such a program may lead to resistance by the existing labor force if it is seen as a threat to their jobs and labor standards.

Use of the public sector to train and hire low-productivity workers has similar advantages and disadvantages. Among the latter are the threat of displacing existing workers, the possibility that the jobs may be unproductive and of the dead-end variety, and the possibility that many of the workers will be inefficient. Private employers are usually under great pressure to let inefficient workers go than is the case with public employers.

Unless efficiency is an overarching goal, some inefficiency can be tolerated—and in practice, it must be tolerated. The wage of the inefficient worker would be, in effect, part transfer payment. It would resemble the mixture of wage income and supplemental relief that is offered by FAP or NIT, (Negative Income Tax) except that the relief component would not be so obvious. Public sector jobs, more than private sector jobs, lend themselves to the application of the "new careers" model. The opportunity to move up a career ladder opens an exit from poverty to those who can take advantage of it.

An expansion of the public sector may be desirable in and of itself, without reference to an antipoverty goal. If such an expansion is sought, the working poor can supply some of the necessary labor, and there is no inherent need for the jobs to be "leaf raking." Government can set an example to the private sector in efforts to restructure jobs so that an upward progression is possible, or so that mothers with small children can more easily hold the jobs.

The two means suggested above—subsidized jobs and government jobs—are more applicable to specific target populations than as general programs. They do not, however, obviate the need for a full employment policy. That condition will always remain necessary to prevent work programs from degenerating into a game of musical chairs.

REDUCTION OF POVERTY IN THE SHORT RUN

The public may want to choose a larger goal—the reduction of poverty. Let us examine this first from a static point of view, and then from a dynamic standpoint.

The means used to achieve the first goal—reduction in dependency -are applicable here if their limits are perceived. A major constraint was the fact that the promotion of employment was applicable only to employables, who just comprise one part of the poverty population. If poverty is defined in the absolute sense, economic growth will translate itself into more jobs and higher pay, some of which will accrue to the employable poor. But there are still those who are beyond the reach of such a solution.

Income Transfers. The search for a means to achieve the goal of reducing poverty leads inevitably to income transfers. Transfers of sufficient size can "eliminate" poverty, by bringing all the poor over the poverty line. No other alternatives exist for those who cannot or should not enter the productive economy.[11] This point needs to be stressed. If a society does not want poverty, it must be prepared to support some of its members at a standard of living that is commonly believed to be non-poor.

Given a substantial income-transfer program, some conflict among goals must be examined. The existence of income transfers may reduce work incentives. If this situation is overcome by introducing negative tax-type incentives into the transfer, then costs are raised. The higher the minimum guaranteed income, the greater the cost. The stronger the incentive is, the greater the cost will be. The combination of a high minimum and a strong incentive (low offsetting tax rate) creates a considerable overspill of benefits into the non-poor segment of the population. It is necessary to face this dilemma in order to understand the real implications of a policy when political rhetoric may be clouding the issue. For instance, FAP may be a desirable policy in its own right, but the low minimum ($1,600 for a family of four) and high offsetting tax rate (50 percent) mean that eliminating poverty is not even a remote possibility.

Necessary Elements of the Policy. An antipoverty policy, in the static sense, should consist of the elements we have described above: income transfers; training and other human capital endowments, together with supportive services such as child care centers; better functioning labor markets—which includes the removal of racial barriers to employment, provisions for feeding trainees into jobs, with possible resort to guaranteed jobs, relocation allowances, and better information about job vacancies; and full employment so that, in the aggregate, jobs are available. Some of these elements may conflict with each other and with other goals that the society may have. Where this is the case, some reasonable compromise must be made. It may, for example, be desirable to give up some price stability in order to obtain higher levels of employment. Or it might be cheaper and more humane to rely on incentives rather than on compulsion. Compulsion satisfies the society's work ethic but may alienate the poor and help to perpetuate social divisions within the community. Points of compromise are ultimately a matter of political determination.

REDUCTION OF POVERTY IN THE LONG RUN

The society's goal might be to reduce or eliminate poverty in a dynamic sense, so that the pattern of poverty is not repeated in each generation. This means dealing with the causes of poverty, rather than merely with its manifestations. This puts us on less firm ground insofar as knowledge goes, but we can point to the directions which hold the most promise.

To begin with, the static policies associated with the reduction of poverty are necessary, as a first step. But some members of the poverty population are beyond rescue into the world of work. They are too old, too infirm, too uneducated, too inexperienced or too alienated. The aim of a dynamic policy is to prevent or minimize this phenomenon in future generations.

For this purpose the distribution of income should be altered in the direction of greater equality. ("Income" is used here in the sense of a claim on both public and private goods.) The method is to make both taxes and public expenditures more progressive. The effect of this would be to reduce the economic distance between those at the bottom of the income distribution pile and the rest of the population. From a relative point of view, this is the only feasible method of attack on poverty.

The intent of this strategy is not merely to alter the shape of the income distribution pattern, but also to change the probability of being at the bottom. Better housing, health and education, delivered in a setting where inequality is less pronounced, can give the children of the poor a better chance to compete, so that they will not be doomed to carry forward disadvantages of their parents.

Even under ideal conditions, there will be people in need of aid. In any economic system, capitalist, socialist, or even feudal, there are those who, for a variety of reasons, have no productive resources to offer. Hence, income transfers will always be necessary.

An economic analysis of poverty and public assistance touches more issues than can be covered adequately in a work of this nature. Although the poor are largely outside the mainstream of economic activity, they are affected by decisions that are not intended to have reference to them. Hence, the economics of poverty is linked to urban economics, to labor economics, agricultural economics, and to fiscal and monetary policy. And economics offers only a partial view of poverty; all the sciences that deal with human behavior have something to contribute.

Analysis may be useful in the design of effective antipoverty programs, but it is not a substitute for action. Furthermore, the poverty analyst, even within the confines of academia, cannot restrict his analyses to the poor. The behavior of the non-poor also needs to be examined. Recommendations for action must be addressed to them, or to those among them who have the power to change things.

It is perfectly obvious that something can be done about poverty. Even if poverty is seen as a relative matter, the lot of those at the bottom can be improved, and their children need not be condemned to repeat the cycle. We have seen that measures to help the poor present problems, but none of the problems is insuperable, especially when one stops expecting perfect solutions to human problems.

To do something substantial requires an act of political

will, since some resources must be transferred from the affluent to the poor. This sacrifice need not be very great. Indeed, the narrowing of the effective range of income inequality can produce benefits to the general public in the form of public services that the general public needs and wants. Poverty can be attacked with relatively little economic pain.

Whether or not such political will is present remains to be seen. As of 1970, the electorate seemed to be disenchanted with antipoverty efforts. Other expenditures, including the Indo-China conflict, appeared to have a greater claim on the public purse. Yet, poverty remains enough of a nagging issue to be reflected in legislation such as the Revenue Act of 1969 and the family assistance act,

This nation's socioeconomic system generates poverty as a by-product of its affluence. Those who have few or no productive resources to offer are discarded like "no return" bottles; others are not given the opportunity to acquire these resources. Still others, who have productive powers, find that they cannot sell them on equal terms with the majority. I speak here not only of racial discrimination, but also of discrimination against women and those aged people who are willing and able to work. In analogous fashion, the economy generates pollution as a by-product of its remarkable ability to produce goods and services.

It is my personal view that the production of poverty is morally offensive, but in deference to the value-free traditions of economics, I shall not impose this value judgment on the reader. Instead, I shall suggest that poverty is a form of pollution. It spoils the quality of life for the non-poor as well as for the poor. The city resident knows this, and the suburban resident fears it. Perhaps the rising concern with the environment will again direct the public's attention toward poverty. In that case, the public may come to place a higher value on the benefits derived from a substantial alleviation of poverty. If the poor do not wait this long, then social disorder can be expected, probably in the form of racial disturbances. The poor cannot win at this game, but they can impose substantial costs on the general public. It would be a pity if the key to antipoverty action lay in violence.

NOTES

1. Joseph Pechman, "The Rich, the Poor and the Taxes They Pay," *Public Interest*, no. 17 (Fall 1969): 24n.

2. William G. Spady, "Educational Mobility and Access: Growth and Paradoxes," *American Journal of Sociology* 73, no. 3 (November 1967): 277.

3. S. M. Miller and Pamela Roby, *The Future of Inequality* (New York: Basic Books, 1970), p. 133.

4. U.S. Department of Health, Education, and Welfare, *Toward a Social Report* (Washington, D.C.: U.S. Government Printing Office 1969), pp. 22–24.

5. More precisely, to the point where the marginal social costs equal the marginal social benefits to the rule-making group.

6. For a theoretical discussion of this tactic, see Peter S. Albin and Bruno Stein, "The Constrained Demand for Public Assistance," *Journal of Human Resources* 3, no. 3 (Summer 1968): 300–11.

7. Lester C. Thurow, *Poverty and Discrimination* (Washington: Brookings Institution, 1969), pp. 139–44.

8. For a fuller discussion of this problem, see ibid., pp. 173–86.

9. The basic economic theory on the topic is Gary S. Becker, *The Economics of Discrimination* (Chicago: University of Chicago Press, 1957), where the subject is treated as an exercise in international trade theory. For an important critique of thes approach, see Thurow, Poverty, pp. 112–26.

10. For a discussion of this point, see U.S. Congress, *Family Assistance Act of 1970*, Hearings before the Committee on Finance, U.S. Senate, 91st Congress, 2nd Session of H.R. 16311, Part I, (April 29,30, and May 1, 1970): pp. 254–55.

11. Others have reached the same, if obvious, conclusion. See especially Thomas I. Ribich, *Education and Poverty* (Washington: Brookings Institution, 1968), p. 116, and Thurow, *Poverty*, pp. 151–52.

Postscript: Elder's Lib
New York Times

The elderly now represent 10 percent of the population of the United States, cast more than 15 percent of the vote and are growing fast enough to command major political attention. No doubt these facts account for the emphasis on action instead of rhetoric at the current White House Conference on Aging, the second of its kind. Arthur S. Flemming, its chairman, wants the emphasis to fall on the older citizen's "inadequacy of income"—a mild phrase, considering that one fourth of all Americans over 65 are forced to live on a poverty-level income, as defined by the Department of Labor. Many more must make do on fixed incomes little above that level while wrestling with inflationary prices, rising property taxes, wretched transportation systems and even nursing homes that it would take a Dickens to excoriate adequately.

The five-day conference is expected to deal with these issues, but little can be hoped for unless it comes to grips with Mr. Flemming's salient point. It is nothing short of scandalous that the recent boost in Social Security payments has meant for many elderly not more income, but less. Increased payments from this source have, under varying state regulations, automatically cut off thousands from Medicaid, hospitalization insurance, welfare assistance and even food stamps. Yet they are forced to take this "raise" which leaves them substantially worse off than they were.

An injustice of far longer standing is the penalty of reduced Social Security payments for those who exceed low annual limit of $1,680 in earned income, while no such penalty is invoked against those well off enough to collect dividends from investments. Perhaps most urgent of all, education and possibly legislation are needed to end arbitrary discrimination based on a fixed age—for employment and various types of license—rather than on a person's physical and mental state.

In this age of self-liberators, the aging should certainly not let themselves be forgotten.

December 1, 1971

Contributors

Jerome M. Comar is president of the Jewish Federation of Metropolitan Chicago.

Paul Cowan writes for *The Village Voice*. He is the author of *The Making of an Un-American.*

Phyllis Franck is a descendant of a Hasidic family.

Martin Hochbaum is assistant director of the commission on urban affairs, American Jewish Congress.

Leo Jung is a rabbi, educator and author. He has written numerous books, including *Essentials of Judaism* and is the editor of *The Jewish Library.*

William Kavesh is a doctor in Cambridge, Massachusetts.

Naomi Levine is national executive director of the American Jewish Congress.

Sol Levy is executive director of a YM-YWHA in Brooklyn, New York.

Oscar Lewis was professor of anthropology at the University of Illinois. He authored many scholarly articles and books including *Children of Sanchez.*

Aviva Silberman has been active in social welfare research and programming in Chicago.

Bruno Stein is a professor of economics at New York University. He is the author of numerous articles on labor economics and the economics of welfare.

Isadore Twersky is the Nathan Littauer Professor of Hebrew Literature and Philosophy at Harvard University. His books include *Rabad of Posquieres* and *A Study of Maimonides*.

Bernard Weinberger is a rabbi and assistant administrator in New York City's Human Resources Administration.

Ann G. Wolfe is the social welfare consultant for the American Jewish Committee. She is the author of several articles that have appeared in professional journals.

Index

Akiba, R., 73, 74, 75, 76
American Jewish Congress, 140
Baron, Salo, 28–29
Chesed, 73, 74–75
Council of Jewish Federations and Welfare Funds, 29, 168, 170, 175
Crown Heights, 141
Cuba, 18, 19
Culture of poverty causes, 10–12
    class consciousness, 17
    community spirit, 15
    distribution in United States, 21
    future of, 23, 24
    major traits, 16–17
    means of studying, 13
    positive aspects, 21–23
Daily Forward, 57
Dana, Herman, 169
Economic Opportunity Act, 135, 137, 138, 143–44
Family Assistance Plan, 188, 191–92, 193, 195
Fanon, Frantz, 19, 20
Federation of Jewish Philanthropies of New York, 2, 3, 104

Harrington, Michael, 9, 26
Jewish college freshmen, parents' income, 1
Jewish community organization, 36–37
Jewish Federation of Metropolitan Chicago, 113, 115, 118
Jewish hospitals
    justification, 168–74
    community control, 176–77
Jewish poor
    job training, 157–60
    Lower East Side, 40–58
    New York City, 2, 34, 39
    Philadelphia, 34–35
    problems of, 3–5, 32, 110, 118–21, 157–58, 160–62
    size, 36, 108–9, 135–36, 157
Jewish population in America, 27
    age, 29–30, 32–33
    future growth, 30
    income, 31
    source of growth, 28
Jewish Week, 26
Jews, Hasidic, 4, 36
    economy, 61
    employment problems, 60–61, 68, 158

European origins, 62
identity crisis, 59–60
Israel of Moldavia, 62
research problems, 64, 65
Sabbath, 64
unifying factors, 67
view of other Jews, 63
Mexico, 20, 21
Mt. Sinai Hospital, 168, 178
National Opinion Research
Survey, 31, 32
Negative income tax, 191, 193
New York City Community
Development Agency, 148,
150, 164
New York City Council Against
Poverty, 137–38, 144, 146,
147, 149, 150
New York City Human Re-
sources Administration, 39–
40, 142, 146
Office of Economic Opportu-
nity, 140
Older Americans, 200
Open hiring, 130–31
Poor, nature of, 9–10
definition, 105–6
Poverty v. the culture of
poverty, 17–18
Poverty program,
reasons for low Jewish

participation, 136–43,
151–52, 154–56
Poverty, concern of non-poor,
185–87
Public assistance eligibility,
188–89
Public assistance recipients and
job training, 189–91
Puerto Rico, 20–21
Puerto Rican Community Development Project, 137

Racial and Ethnic Balance Plan,
144–45
Sanhedrin 100, 101
San Juan, 15–16, 20
Scheuer, Congressman, 139, 149
Social Security, 111, 201
South Africa, 12–13
South Beach, 3, 32
Stuyvesant, Peter, 102–3, 107
Turnus, Rufus, 73, 75, 76
Tzedakah, 73
aged, 89
handouts, 96–97
loans, 97–98
motive, 78
preventive, 99–100
Weinberger, Bernard, 65–66
White House Conference on
Aging, 200
Williamsburg, 36, 59, 63, 158